LAND REFORM IN LATIN AMERICA

LAND REFORM
IN LATIN AMERICA

The Dominican Case

CARRIE A. MEYER

PRAEGER

New York
Westport, Connecticut
London

Library of Congress Cataloging-in-Publication Data

Meyer, Carrie A.
Land reform in Latin America : the Dominican case / Carrie A.
Meyer.
p.   cm.
Bibliography: p.
ISBN 0-275-93202-8 (alk. paper)
1. Land reform—Dominican Republic. 2. Agriculture—Economic
aspects—Dominican Republic.   I. Title.
HD1333.D65M49   1989
333.3'1'7293—dc19   88-39661

Library of Congress Catalog Card Number: 88-39661
ISBN: 0-275-93202-8

First published in 1989

Praeger Publishers, One Madison Avenue, New York, NY 10010
A division of Greenwood Press, Inc.

Printed in the United States of America

The paper used in this book complies with the
Permanent Paper Standard issued by the National
Information Standards Organization (Z39.48-1984).

10 9 8 7 6 5 4 3 2 1

To the rural Dominicans who opened their hearts and homes to me as a Peace Corps volunteer and as a researcher

Contents

Illustrations

Tables

Preface

As a study of land reform, the major focus of this book is reform project organization. A general survey of agrarian reform in Latin America is first made to bring out the common problems and questions of organizational structure. Then, those questions found to be of general relevance are explored more fully as the study is narrowed to agrarian reform in the Dominican Republic.

I wish to thank Professors Werner Baer, Lanny Arvan, Hadi Esfahani, and Michael Carter for their assistance in reading and criticizing the rough drafts of this work. I am indebted to the Tinker Foundation for financial support for field research, to David Stanfield for his inspiration and many contacts in the Dominican Republic, to Dan Biller for proofreading, to George Mason University Office Support Services for preparation of page proofs, and particularly to the many Dominicans who made this work possible: the Reyes family, the Pérez family, César Mejía, Carlos Dore, Benito Ferreiras, José Sicard, Luis Castro, Gumesindo Gómez, and Guarín, to name only a few. All errors and omissions are my own.

Introduction and Overview

Land reform has long been a central issue in Latin American development economics. Saddled with extreme inequality of land distribution from their colonial roots, the countries of Latin America have struggled to overcome political crises and stagnation in their road to development. Land reform has been heralded by numerous scholars and development economists, as well as by revolutionaries, as the essential ingredient for economic growth. The U.S. policy in Latin America under the Alliance for Progress in the early 1960s pushed for land reform along with their aid packages, and reform occurred in a number of countries throughout the 1960s and 1970s. Results have, however, been disappointing, at least in terms of measurable productivity increases. In most cases ambiguous or even negative changes have been registered and the obvious question is, Why?

Land reform has been motivated in large part by macroeconomic goals: political stabilization, improved labor absorption, and increased consumer demand by expansion of peasant income. But perhaps in its enthusiasm, land reform may break down the existing institutional network without erecting an appropriate structure for efficient production. The purpose of this study is to analyze some of the microeconomic details that underlie the inadequate performance of reform sector agriculture.

The Dominican Republic is chosen as a case in particular that is not atypical of agrarian reforms in general in Latin America.

Agrarian reform in the Dominican Republic has had particular impact in the rice sector, where agrarian reform lands produce close to half of the rice in the country. Like many countries in Latin America, the Dominican Republic has from time to time shifted its strategy between individual and collectively organized reform projects. Within the rice sector, land had been expropriated to individual beneficiaries as well as to collective units. Interestingly, many of the individual beneficiaries have associated themselves for purposes of credit, input purchases, rice marketing, and capital equipment. At the same time, collectives have divided their land into individual parcels and have insisted that the government legalize their "associative" management structure. The "associatives" were in fact legalized in 1985, after most of the collectives had already broken down in 1983.

Recent cases studies of particular agrarian reform projects in the Dominican Republic are used in this study to provide the insight and necessary empirical foundation for analytical research dealing specifically with the organizational structure of the reform project itself. Finally, an empirical evaluation is made of the success of the change to the associative structure by the reform projects in the rice sector in the Dominican Republic.

The study proceeds as follows:

Chapter 1 provides a comprehensive survey of the issues surrounding agrarian reform projects in Latin America to serve as the theoretical foundation for the study. Empirical detail from countries that have undertaken reforms is provided in an attempt to assess the various project management forms.

The Dominican Republic is introduced in Chapter 2 with a brief review of its history, land settlement, and the role that agriculture plays in its economy.

Chapter 3 focuses on agrarian reform in the Dominican Republic. The history of the reform and the institutional framework is first developed before restricting attention to the rice sector and its particular context. The local debate on the appropriate organizational structure is presented, as well as efforts to evaluate the collective and individual structures. Finally, case studies of particular reform projects document aspects of their functioning, such as administrative structure, agency participation, credit problems, and capital investment.

The literature relevant to an analytical study of the organizational structure of reform sector projects is reviewed briefly in Chapter 4. This includes an introduction to major bodies of literature on contracts and organization in microeconomic theory, including principal-agent, team theory, and hierarchies and supervision, as well as the literature dealing with contracts in agriculture from the experience in the Soviet Union, China, India, and Southeast Asia.

Chapter 5 constitutes the major original contribution of the study. Formal analytical models are developed to explore the implications of the individual, collective, and associative organizational structures of land reform projects. Mathematical proofs are used to show the pareto superiority of the associative form over both the individual and the collective forms of organization.

Finally, in Chapter 6, an evaluation of the movement to the associative structure in the rice areas of the agrarian reform sector in the Dominican Republic is made. This draws on the reaction of the local leaders of the reform projects, as well as on empirical data on the productivity per hectare achieved before and after the change in organizational structure, at both the local and national levels.

1

The Development and Organization of Land Reform in Latin America

Although the heyday of the land reform era in Latin America has come and gone with disappointing results, the structural imbalances that have prompted the cry for land reform in the past have yet to be alleviated. As we are reminded by the more recent reforms in El Salvador and Nicaragua, both sides of the political spectrum recognize the need to include agrarian reform in their political agenda.

The agrarian structure of Latin America is characterized by the extreme concentration of landholdings in the hands of a few—the *latifundios*—alongside the landholdings too small to maintain the families living on them—the *minifundios*. Both of these extremes are generally considered inefficient (Barraclough 1973; Carroll 1961; Figueroa 1977; Furtado 1976): the *latifundios* for their idle land, absentee ownership, and monopsony on labor with the *colono* tenant labor system; the *minifundios* for their lack of investment and long-term planning and susceptibility to overuse and erosion. Because of such unequal land distribution, the question of land reform is an obvious one and its political motivation is clear.

The economic case for land reform developed and crystallized in the 1960s and 1970s (Dorner and Kanel 1971; Dovring 1970a). A more equitable distribution of land would provide for a more equitable distribution of income and increased consumer demand to spur development in the rest of the economy. Labor-intensive methods on small farms would absorb the abundant labor and provide the appropriate alternative to the relatively capital-intensive production on large farms in a capital-scarce economy. Productivity per unit of land should increase.

Productivity, understandably, has been a sensitive issue throughout the land reform controversy. Have land reform programs been shown to improve productivity? R. Albert Berry (1984: 80) addresses the question: "At worst, there is no serious ground to fear a decrease in output provided a reform is competently executed and service levels do not deteriorate." The point is made that although output-per-land ratios have been found to vary inversely with size (Kanel 1967) and output-per-labor ratios to vary directly with size, the relationship between total factor productivity and size is unclear. In Bolivia, Berry reports an initial drop and later increases in productivity. In Mexico there were controversial results (Dovring 1970b). While admitting a weakening negative relationship of farm size to factor productivity because large farmers have adapted new technology most rapidly, and stressing the need for complementary government policies (these include extension services, credit, and marketing), Berry remains on the positive side of the productivity question.

The question that this study will tackle, however, is not whether but how. In other words, given that land reform is and will remain a central component of the political scene in Latin America, how is it to be administered? Many have emphasized that land reform is best instituted as a part in an integrated program of rural development. As John Mellor puts it, "Land reform may be a necessary condition of agricultural development but it certainly is not a sufficient condition" (Mellor 1966: 262). Warriner (1973) distinguishes between "simple" and "integral" reform and finds that integral reform has better results in terms of agricultural productivity and capital investment. Adolfo Figueroa, likewise, emphasizes that "land reform realizes its greatest potential when it serves as a framework for other policies" (Figueroa 1977: 155), among which he includes infrastructure; modern inputs such as credit, extension, and research activities; pricing policies; and efforts toward rural industrialization.

Acceptance of the need for these complementary support services has led many countries to organize land reform projects into collectives or production cooperatives. But the disincentives to effort inherent in group farming have been a continual source of underproduction and disappointment with cooperative farming experiments.

This chapter specifically examines the issues involved in the decision to organize the land reform projects in individual, collective, or mixed alternatives. It also focuses on credit issues. Before these issues are addressed, however, a picture of the extent to which agrarian reform has affected Latin America is presented. The chapter then reviews experience with reform projects from various countries in Latin America before drawing to a conclusion.

THE SPECTRUM OF LAND REFORM IN LATIN AMERICA

Agrarian reform, if defined loosely,[1] has affected almost all the countries in Latin America to at least some extent. A few have had no more than colonization programs on virgin land. Many others passed legislation with encouragement from the Alliance for Progress in the early 1960s and expropriated public lands for land reform projects. Several have undergone reforms that have drastically altered the rural institutional framework.

A brief survey of the progress of land reform in 20 countries in Latin America is presented in Table 1.1. As shown in the table, substantial reforms, affecting over 20 percent of the rural population, have occurred in 9 of the 20 countries, although in Chile and especially in Guatemala, these were very short lived. The reforms that have left the most sweeping changes on the rural scene are those of Cuba, Haiti, Bolivia, and Mexico, all of which were the product of revolution.

Often neglected as an example of land reform, Haiti was the first to redistribute land to the masses. In the early nineteenth century, five years after Toussaint L'Ouverture led the slave rebellion to independence in 1804, Pétion began the redistribution of land. Mats Lundahl blames the stagnant subsistence agriculture in Haiti, in part, on the early land reform because it "contributed to an almost hermetic separation of the masses from the elite" (Lundahl 1979: 289). He argues that the ex-slaves were pacified with small parcels of land, and then, without access to land as a means to accrue wealth, the elite turned to politics and the "spoils" of government.

The Mexican revolution of the early twentieth century brought the second major land reform, returning lands to the peasant communities that had been overtaken by the large estates. Guatemala between 1952 and 1954 experienced a massive but very short-lived agrarian reform. Bolivia followed with revolution, and the peasants divided the land up among themselves in 1953. After the Cuban revolution almost all of the remaining countries enacted agrarian reform legislation. And most recently we have seen the reforms of Nicaragua and El Salvador.

Of those countries where land reform has affected over 3 percent of the rural households, all except Haiti and Bolivia have had experience with some kind of production cooperative (coops in Table 1.1). Here production cooperative is defined, as in Dorner and Kanel, "as an organization in which the bulk of the land is held and farmed in common by the group" (Dorner and Kanel 1977: 5). The land may be owned either by the group or the state, and many decisions are made by managers who may be local and/or government agency officials.

Table 1.1

Agrarian Reform Surveyed in Latin America

Country	Reform Period Covered	Percent Rural Households Benefitting[b]	Type of Organization
Argentina	1940-1968	0.8%	Indiv[a]
Bolivia	1953-1975	78.9%	Indiv
Brazil	1964-1969	0.4%	Indiv
Chile	1962-1973	20.0%	*Asentamientos*
counter-ref	1973-1975	4.0%	Indiv
Colombia	1961-1977	8.0%	Indiv; Coops
Costa Rica	1961-1979	13.5%	Indiv; Coops
Cuba	1959-1981	100.0%	State; Indiv; Coops
Dom Rep	1962-1986	19.2%	Indiv; Coops
Ecuador	1964-1976	9.1%	Indiv; Coops
El Salvador	1980-1983	12.0%	Indiv; Coops
Guatemala	1952-1954	33.0%	Indiv; Coops
counter-ref	1954-1969	3.0%	Indiv
Haiti	1809-1883	80.0%	Indiv
Honduras	1962-1980	10.4%	Indiv; Coops
Mexico	1917-1980	52.4%	*Ejidos*
Nicaragua	1979-1983	30.0%	State; Indiv; Coops
Panama	1963-1969	2.7%	Indiv; Coops
Paraguay	1963-1969	6.8%	Indiv[a]
Peru	1967-1979	21.3%	*Empresas Asociativas*
Uruguay	1948-1969	0.5%	Indiv[a]
Venezuela	1959-1975	25.4%	Indiv; Coops

[a] These countries had only colonization projects.

[b] To compute percent rural households benefitting, figures for Economically Active Males in Agriculture were taken from the *UN Demographic Yearbook* using Table 28 in 1984, Tables 38 and 39 in 1979, and Table 10 in 1972. *America en Cifras, 1967,* table 408-02, was the source for Panama. The figure for the Dominican Republic was taken from *R.D. en Cifras*, 1986, p. 284. Where Economically Active Males in Agriculture is not cited in the notes, the figures for percent rural households benefitting were taken directly from the primary sources listed below:

Country	Source	Beneficiaries	Census	Ec Act Males
Argentina	Wilkie, 1974, p.8	9,139	1970	1,218,150
Bolivia	King, 1977, p.118	477,000	1976	604,078
Brazil	Wilkie, 1974, p.3	46,457	1970	11,792,294
Chile	DeJanvry, 1981, p.206			
Colombia	Grindle, 1986, p.136	186,000	1964	2,311,058
Costa Rica	Hall, 1985, p.204	28,079	1973	208,642
Cuba	DeJanvry, 1981, p.206			
Dom Rep	IAD, 1987	72,509	1981	378,274
Ecuador	FAO, 1980, p.93	78,320	1974	856,508
El Salvador	Deere, 1985, p.1039	74,936		
Guatemala	DeJanvry, 1981, p.206			
Haiti	Zuvekas, 1978, p.7			
Honduras	Ruhl, 1984, p.53	46,890	1974	451,982
Mexico	FAO, 1980, p.80	2,600,000	1980	4,957,340
Nicaragua	Deere, 1985, p.1039	72,072		
Panama	Wilkie, 1974, p.3,8	4,085	1960	150,817
Paraguay	Wilkie, 1974, p.8	23,832	1972	350,937
Peru	Kay, 1982, p.152	337,662	1981	1,583,981
Uruguay	Wilkie, 1974, p.8	900	1975	170,600
Venezuela	Cox, 1978, p.8	150,574	1971	593,385

The later sections of this chapter are devoted to a closer look at experiences with various forms of cooperative organizations in a number of these countries. Before examining them, however, the major issues of cooperative farming and small farmer credit are identified in the following two sections.

INDIVIDUAL PARCELS, COLLECTIVE FARMS, AND DEGREES OF COOPERATION: THE ISSUES

Throughout Latin America, with varying degrees of success or failure, government officials have experimented with a wide variety of management models for land reform projects. Experience ranges from parcels allocated to individual families in Bolivia with minimal associated support or services, to the military collective farms in Peru, which have, since their conception, undergone a high degree of decollectivization. Intermediary degrees of cooperation are exemplified by the *ejidos* in Mexico and the *asentamientos* of the Allende reform in Chile.

Hung-Chao Tai claims that "indeed, virtually all people concerned with agricultural development consider it necessary and desirable to integrate the farming community into cooperative societies for purposes of credit provision, marketing, and other services" (Tai 1974: 234). However, according to Barraclough, "In spite of widespread agreement about the desirability of farmers' cooperatives, actual experience has frequently been rather discouraging in Latin America" (Barraclough 1971: 379). This section is devoted to discussing the arguments in favor of and opposed to cooperative farming and addresses the issue of mixed alternatives.

In Support of Cooperation

Perhaps the most overriding argument in support of cooperative rural organizations is the need to provide credit to the small farmer. Otto Schiller says that

> In most cases the credit requirements of small agricultural producers were the main reason for the introduction of a cooperative system in developing countries. The transition from subsistence to money or market economy—one of the preconditions for agricultural progress—requires some capital investment which the small agricultural producer in general cannot materialize out of his own resources. (Schiller 1971: 286)

Likewise Barraclough emphasizes, "There is practically no way of getting credit to millions of landless labourers and very small farmers except through some kind of organization" (Barraclough 1976: 558). Primary advantages to group lending include lower transaction costs for both borrowers and lenders as well as lower costs of supervision and assistance. Further issues of small farmer credit are discussed in the following section.

Another major point in favor of cooperation is that when farmers are organized, it becomes much easier for the government to provide the additional support services, such as extension, marketing, and inputs like seeds and fertilizers (King 1977: 57; Dorner and Kanel 1977: 7). Some argue that without new technology, few profitable alternatives exist for the small farmer, and from this viewpoint technical assistance and modern inputs become essential ingredients for the success of land reform projects (Tinnermeier 1973).

With regard to "internal" economies of scale, there is some debate as to whether cooperative production provides scale benefits. King, citing Dorner and Kanel (1971) and Kanel (1967), says that "according to many authors internal economies of scale in agriculture cease to be important beyond a farm size that fully employs the labour of the family. With regard to external economies (large scale machinery, supply of fertilisers and seeds, credit, processing and marketing) the position is different and usually demands some kind of group action" (King 1977: 57). Even Dorner and Kanel, however, admit that there may be economies of scale in production, especially when considerable infrastructure exists on large estates that have been turned over to the land reform agency or when irrigation is required (Dorner and Kanel 1977: 6). Putterman refers to "the enormous body of evidence suggesting that small farms are more productive, in terms of land and capital, than are large ones" with considerable skepticism, emphasizing that the evidence merely confirms that "different farm sizes are associated with differing factoring proportions" (Putterman 1983: 80-81). Excessive fragmentation is a problem in some areas such as in Haiti, which underwent extensive land reform in the nineteenth century (Zuvekas 1978). Cooperatives may be one way to avoid the fragmentation problem. Certainly it must be remembered that farming enterprises are particularly site-specific among enterprises in general. The appropriate scale will depend on local conditions—especially geography, climate, and crops grown—and will change as technology changes.

Moving away from scale advantages, the potential political advantages to rural organizations, especially increased bargaining power, must be recognized (Barraclough 1971: 365). Many also argue that the human resources available may be better utilized and developed, since organizations "absorb individuals with a wide range of talents and interests" (Dorner and Kanel 1977: 7; Putterman 1983). Scarce managerial skills are economized upon, as well as developed for potential applications in other enterprises.

Problems with Cooperation

However appealing may be the arguments for group farming, as previously mentioned, where it has been tried in Latin America, the results have been disappointing. Barraclough (1971) cites examples of initial success and eventual failure of cooperative farming projects in Chile as well as in most other countries. Most authors agree that the problems encountered center around internal organization of the project and individual incentive.[2] Dorner and Kanel emphasize that these problems are not easily overcome:

> It is a delusion to expect that group farms have such obvious benefits to members or such decisive economic advantages to make it possible to overcome easily the organizational problems. These organizational problems are largely due to ambiguities in roles of both managers and members of group farms. Members are supposed to be both workers and participants in policy-making; managers are supposed to supervise the workers and at the same time to be responsible to them. (Dorner and Kanel 1977: 8)

They find that these ambiguities result in poor management and slack effort by members and suggest that the problems should be approached by recognizing that the state and members have divergent interests. The state would reportedly be interested in increasing total production, increasing investment—perhaps by restricting consumption, maintaining equal opportunity among the rural population, and increasing their base of political support. Members would be interested in income and services provided by the group farm, opportunities for individual initiative and advancement, "as well as possibilities for engaging in at least some private family farming" (Dorner and Kanel 1977: 10). Dorner and Kanel add that the dichotomy of interests between members and the state reveals the difficulty the manager would have as a liaison between them. It should also be recognized that the manager must be expected to have his own personal interest at heart when performing his role.

Tai also emphasizes the problem of management—in particular the problem of choosing a manager: "If the cultivators choose their manager from among themselves, he frequently does not have the administrative and technical competence to run a large farm. If they select a competent outsider as the manager, they lose even more the sense of ownership of their pooled land" (Tai 1974: 235-36). Barraclough, along a similar line, criticizes government officials who "manage things too much." He continues, "It appears to most officials easier and more efficient to build cooperatives from the top down instead of from the bottom up as the latter course requires patient and skillful educational and promotional efforts" (Barraclough 1971: 383). An alternative might be for the government to provide management in the initial stages while training a member who could then take over the task.

A final point brought up by Michael Carter is that alongside the internal problems of management and incentives, "large scale cooperative producers are vulnerable to external manipulation and may experience extrinsically caused productivity problems" (Carter 1984a: 3). He refers to policies, imposed upon the cooperative, that may be considered socially desirable but reduce cooperative profitability, as well as a lack of flexibility in responding to adverse market conditions.

Degrees of Cooperation

In fact, the choice of individual or group farming is not one of "either/or" but one of degree. Warriner, after weighing the pros and cons of the cooperative and individual farming alternatives, admits that the best tenure arrangement is really an unknown (and, one might add, specific to local conditions). She then emphasizes, "But we should do well to get away from the concept of simple individualism and pure collectivism as mutually exclusively alternatives; in all rural societies there are individual and collective functions" (Warriner 1973: 124-25). Boguslaw Galeski (1977) classifies cooperative enterprises according to a continuum of increasing socialization of ownership and production.

Dr. Otto Schiller is one who promotes the idea of trying to capture the benefits of both extremes. He recognizes the desire for individual ownership of land and suggests that "the question is, therefore, to what extent the advantages of cooperative action in farming operations can also be realized, if individual use of land is maintained (Schiller 1969: 48). Putterman (1983), rather than hoping to add cooperative benefits to individual farming, promotes the contrary, that is, capturing individual incentive with private family garden plots, in an essentially collective model. His model describes a common feature of the reform sector in Latin America and has met with varied success. Michael Carter, in regard to the coastal agricultural production cooperatives in Peru undergoing parcellation, asks a different question: "Can different stages of production be differentially organized, with appropriate scale and incentive devices applied to each?" He suggests using parcellation as a piece-rate incentive device while maintaining collective property rights under a system where "the individual's income would . . . be composed of time-based wages, a fixed responsibility share, plus incentive payments" (Carter 1984a: 7-8). David Stanfield and others have studied the transformation of land reform projects in the Dominican Republic and find that both individual and collective units have moved toward an intermediate type of management form "based on individual responsibilities for a particular piece of land, but with certain activities carried out by the *campesinos* as a group" (Stanfield et al. 1983: 3).

Unquestionably the appropriate alternative cannot be determined without a case in point. After first surveying the experience in general in Latin America, we focus on the case of the Dominican Republic in an attempt to lay the foundation for the theoretical modeling that follows.

CREDIT TO THE SMALL FARMER: THE ISSUES

Credit, cooperatives, and agrarian reform together made up the core of rural development programs in Latin America in the 1960s and 1970s.

Unfortunately, there has been no less disappointment with credit programs than with the other two. Dale Adams describes cheap credit as perhaps the rotten apple that spoiled the whole bag of rural development efforts over the last three decades:

> Offering cheap credit is a way of enticing people to do business with an organization. . . . If large amounts of funds are available for lending, the credit operations may swamp the other activities of the organization. An agrarian-reform institution may become primarily a supervised credit agency, a multipurpose cooperative may evolve into largely a lending agency, and the staff of extension programs may end up doing mostly loan collection. (Adams 1984: 16-17)

While perhaps not deserving the entire blame, the role of credit as a central factor in agrarian reform needs to be developed.

Credit for Production and as Insurance

Credit plays two very important roles for the small farmer, that of working capital and that of an insurance substitute. The adoption of new technology involving fertilizer, pesticides, hybrid seeds, and capital equipment requires credit up front to be paid off at harvest. Equally important, however, is the role of continuing credit to take the place of insurance in the rural economy. Binswanger and Sillers (1983) document the universal risk aversion of farmers in developing countries and develop the role of credit as an insurance substitute.

According to C. B. Baker, the credit programs could learn some lessons from the local moneylender, especially with respect to the role of credit as an insurance device:

> If the small farmer perceives the SFCP [small farmer credit program] to be culturally ill-adapted, he will view it as temporary and therefore valueless to him as a reserve. Two results follow, both exceedingly damaging. (1) He may consider default to be an acceptable behavior. He will "get his" while the SFCP *is* there. He will return to the moneylender after the SFCP has departed. (2) He may consider the temporary advantages gained in the new program to be outweighed by damage done to his line of credit with the moneylender. Moneylender credit is permanent and versatile, however costly it may be to borrow from the moneylender. SFCP credit is fleeting and questionable, however rewarding it may be in the short run to borrow from the SFCP lending agency. (Baker 1973: 52-53)

For the insurance role of credit, that of a permanent reliable reserve and for financing consumption, the moneylender has decided advantages; but for financing production and marketing, he is not so flexible. Informal lending costs may be as high as 50 to 100 percent, making it very difficult for new technology to pay off. Additionally, the farmer must sell his produce at harvest, when prices are their lowest, to repay the moneylender (Baker 1973: 45-46). Finally, small local lenders cannot deal as efficiently with risk as can institutional lenders, and this increases their rates. According to Lipton, "Small lenders, being localized, suffer major covariance among returns from their loans—if a bad harvest makes some borrowers default, so will other borrowers" (Lipton 1976: 549).

The Problem of Cheap Credit

There now seems to be general agreement that while once seen as essential for rural development, "cheap credit" has undermined rural development efforts (Adams, Graham, and Von Pischke 1984). Baker states:

> There is ample evidence . . . to suggest that low interest rates are damaging to legitimate objectives of the SFCP [small farmer credit program]. They produce a "portfolio shift" toward large farmers, . . . thus thwarting objectives centered on small farmers. They generate on the part of all borrowers an expectation that the SFCP will be temporary, thus producing through default a self-fulfilling prophecy. They generate suboptimal choices by the borrower in his production, marketing and consumption plan. (Baker 1973: 55)

Ultimately, then, cheap credit has been an expensive proposition without the desired results, leading to underproductive investment and distorted consumption spending.

The Credit-Extension Package

Many have argued that extension service must be provided along with credit for the small farmer if it is to be effective. Tinnermeier (1973), in "Technology, Profit, and Agricultural Credit," makes the case that given the existing technology, even with credit available, few profitable alternatives exist for the small farmer. He maintains that extension services are essential to the effective adoption of new technology and that without technical assistance available, credit would have no impact. He adds that farmers organizations would reduce the cost of effectively reaching a large number of small farmers.

Baker, on the other hand, is more skeptical of the "credit in a package" programs. He finds them to be very expensive to run—often breaking the credit program—as well as being extremely bureaucratized, to the extent that they are under suspicion by the small farmer. He admits, however, that "small farmer credit may be successful as a small component in some other infrastructure reform, . . . given proper conditions. It seldom is successful as the principal carrier of wider infrastructure reform" (Baker 1973: 44). Yet many have maintained that land reform is the proper "principal carrier" to serve as a framework for services such as credit and technical assistance (Figueroa 1977).

Administrative Aspects

In the collected papers of the *1973 AID Spring Review of Small Farmer Credit*, Jerome French examines 27 credit programs in 22 countries in an effort to critique their organizational aspects. His principal findings are that, first, external factors, particularly access to land, may restrict the effectiveness of the programs, and without corollary programs, the credit programs may be of questionable value. Second, he finds the need for considerable organizational improvement (French 1973: 237). He suggests that more attention should be focused on the administrative aspects of the programs, that efforts should be made to "work towards . . . simplification of procedures and increased decentralization of operation authority," as well as to "increase direct contact between credit organization personnel, personnel of organizations supplying other inputs, and the small farmers themselves" (French 1973: 247).

Finally, group credit is seen by many as the only way to reach many small farmers at a reasonable cost.[3] Primary advantages of group credit include lower transaction costs for both borrower and lender, as well as the opportunity for technical assistance and supervision at a lower cost. Thomas Carroll stresses, "Leadership and management at all levels of group credit associations are key elements in success." He continues, "Experience shows that there is an extremely delicate relationship between the success of local credit groups . . . and the role of the government." However, as with production cooperatives, he finds that "local leadership . . . is frequently the keystone determining the success or failure of the group" (Carroll 1973: 271, 273). Again we see cause to analyze carefully the distinct roles of the government agency, the local manager, and the small farmer or land reform beneficiary.

EJIDOS IN MEXICO

The example of the *ejidos* in Mexico provides some of the most extensive experience with collective and cooperative farming on land reform projects in Latin America. Instigated not by the prodding of some foreign superpower, the Mexican land reform was born of a bloody peasant revolution. The *ejidos* were a return of lands to the indigenous communal land-holding system, which had been usurped by the large estates, not the product of the latest fad in development circles at the time. Given even these auspicious beginnings, the experience in Mexico has been disappointing.

Redistribution of land began with the new constitution of 1917, but it was not until the period of Lázaro Cárdenas (1934-40) that massive redistribution took place. Since that time the process has been much more gradual, depending upon the biases of the controlling regime. The change effected over the long run has been tremendous—before the revolution it is estimated that only 1 percent of the population owned 97 percent of the land, while 1 percent of the land was owned by 96 percent of the rural population.[4] Since that time, the land reform has come to affect over 50 percent of the land and rural population.[5] Certainly the social and political, as well as economic, implications of such a redistribution of land and power are overwhelming. Whether or not the organizational structure of the *ejidos* was such as to provide the incentives for efficient production is perhaps not the essential question. It is, however, the one to which we address ourselves.

Numerous studies exist that compare productivity in the reform and private sectors in Mexico, and controversy abounds. Unfortunately, the economic issues are often clouded by ideological biases. Folke Dovring, in a noteworthy study published in 1970, attributes lower *ejido* output to land-quality differences and high capital inputs on private farms and maintains that "the sociopolitical gains of the land reform have in no way been at the expense of economic progress" (Dovring 1970b: 274). Edmundo Flores (1970: 904) emphasizes that "political stability, high rates of capital formation, and increased agricultural production and productivity would have been impossible without the land reform." Serious incentive problems, on the other hand, inherent in the *ejidos*, are noted by even the most ardent supporters of land reform.[6] And there are equally many studies that show lower productivity on *ejido* lands.

Ejido lands are communally owned and may be farmed either collectively or in individual plots. Although during the Cárdenas period there was a major movement in support of collective *ejidos*, most *ejidos* are now farmed individually, with centralized credit and marketing.[7] *Ejido* holdings should not be bought or sold, mortgaged, or rented; but in practice much reconcentration has occurred. Stavenhagen (1973: 8) notes a 1966 field survey in Michoacán, in which "55% of all ejidatarios were renting their 10-hectare plots of irrigated land to non-ejido agricultural entrepreneurs."

The *ejido* community is governed by a board of directors, and here Stavenhagen describes the crucial role of the president of the board:

> The president of the board is the key political personality in the ejido and occupies a powerful position. He handles all matters pertaining to ejido land tenure; deals with public agencies; manages the ejido's collective resources and properties; resolves individual tenure problems and conflicts, and so forth. He is not only accountable to the assembly of ejidatarios, but also to the federal agrarian agencies which may demand his removal in case he does not comply with official directives. An ejido president can play an important role in the development of his community, but he can also use his position for personal advantage. Unfortunately, the latter has been more frequently the case than the former, and there are innumerable cases in which ejido leaders have remained in power for many years and have obtained profits for themselves and their friends, disregarding the community's collective needs. Often, they have been able to do so in agreement with outside economic interests and corrupt government officials. (Stavenhagen 1973: 9)

Stavenhagen implies that if only these administrators were less selfishly motivated, the system could be better. It would seem more reasonable, however, to capitalize on the selfish motivation of the individuals in the system with an organizational structure that takes that as an assumption, rather than counting on the altruism of the local leaders and government officials.

With regard to provision of credit to the *ejidatarios*, in 1936 the Banco Nacional de Crédito Ejidal was established for this particular purpose. Although other agricultural credit banks were already in existence, the fact that *ejido* land could not be used as collateral made this special institution necessary. Alan Costa describes the paternalistic role of the bank as follows:

> The Banco Ejidal directs and controls agricultural work on ejidos which are recipients of loans, provides advice on crops to be grown, inspects crops during the growing season, and supervises the use of credit extended. The Banco Ejidal further assists the ejidal sector in purchasing farm machinery and farm supplies, such as seed, fertilizer, and insecticides. Finally, the commercial department of the bank often receives and sells the crop for which the loan was extended. . . . Indeed little decision-making authority remains in the hands of ejidatarios once they opt to obtain credit from the ejidal bank. (Costa 1977: 49)

To receive credit, Costa explains, the *ejidatarios* must form a credit society through which loans are made to individual members; however, each member has unlimited liability for the loans of the society (Costa 1977: 48). When addressing himself to the credit societies, Stavenhagen again emphasizes the important role of the local leader, citing an example in which two credit societies within the same *ejido* experienced dramatically contrasted economic performance due to the personal characteristics of their leadership (Stavenhagen 1973: 16-17).

In general the consensus seems to agree that the collective *ejidos* have had even more severe organizational and incentive problems than the individual *ejidos*.[8] Shlomo Eckstein, in an analysis of the collective, semi-collective, and individual *ejidos* in 88 of Mexico's 2340 counties, concludes that where collective *ejidos* were endowed with adequate resources, irrigation, credit, and technical assistance, they performed more efficiently than did individual *ejidos* under similar conditions; whereas when neither had adequate resources, the individual *ejidos* performed better (Eckstein 1971: 299). Other studies, such as the following, have not supported these results.

In a recent study of collective *henequén ejidos* in the Yucatán, Brannon and Baklanoff report a deplorable situation. The collective *ejidos* there, chosen as models under the Cárdenas administration, had been provided with extensive credit and technical assistance. They explain, however, that "despite the extensive support given the collective experiment in Yucatán, the henequén *ejidos* have virtually become wards of the federal government. Productivity and output have declined significantly below pre-reform levels and the agricultural labour force has been allowed to expand far beyond the actual needs of the industry." They continue to say that bank officials have been making operating and investment decisions and that "*ejidatarios* have come to consider the credit advances as wages to which they are entitled. Because there is no incentive for the *ejidatario* to perform his work efficiently, he often devotes as little time as possible to his weekly tasks, or simply does not do them at all" (Brannon and Baklanoff 1984: 1131-32, 1135).

Finally, Alan Costa has done a study in the Mexican Pacific-North in an attempt to evaluate on a comparative basis the efficiency of small private holders, individual *ejidatarios*, and collective *ejidos*. While the study was undertaken under agricultural conditions of uniformly high quality, his "findings support the hypothesis that economic efficiency wanes as the degree of attenuation of property rights becomes more pronounced" (Costa 1977: 138). Costa attributes some of the success of the private holders, interestingly, to the existence of associations of private agriculturists. He reports that these associations provide services such as marketing, collective purchase of inputs, a credit union, and legal services (Costa 1977: 86).

ASENTAMIENTOS IN CHILE

In contrast to Mexico, agrarian reform in Chile began under the watchful, hopeful eye of the entire "aid community," whose hopes were dashed with a counter-reform only six years after the Agrarian Reform Law (No. 16,640) was passed. The experience, however, provides some useful lessons.

Agrarian reform was initiated under the Christian Democratic government of Eduardo Frei (1964-70) with the intent of increasing agricultural production to provide for the urban population while redistributing income and employment to the rural poor. In 1970, Socialist Salvador Allende was elected promising a "transition to socialism" and in two years expropriated over twice as many farms as had Frei in six years (Castillo and Lehmann 1983: 256). But a military government assumed power in 1973, dismantled most of the *asentamientos*, and distributed the land to individuals, returning much of it to its former owners. Thiesenhusen (1984: 50) reports that under the Frei and Allende regimes, 43 percent of the agricultural land in the country had been expropriated, but 28 percent of that was returned to the original owners with the 1973 coup. Another 5 percent was sold at auction and 10 percent retained for public use; in addition, many of the land reform parcels were resold to large farmers.

According to Castillo and Lehmann, the Frei government had three choices in carrying out the reform:

> redistribute parcels of land from the great estates primarily to the landless . . . . direct its attention to the *minifundistas* . . . [or] seek to transform the estates into some form of co-operative and thus avoid as far as possible a disruption of the technical conditions of production, while redistributing the fruits of that production. (Castillo and Lehmann 1983: 249-50)

The latter course was the one chosen: The estates were left more or less intact and the beneficiaries were to be the former permanent workers. *Asentamientos*, intended as a three- to five-year transitional arrangement, were set up under the direction of the Agrarian Reform Corporation (CORA). The corporation retained possession of the land during this time and contributed credit, gave technical assistance, and held veto power on the administrative council of elected members.

The *asentamientos* experienced a number of major problems, foremost of which, according to Jacques Chonchol (1977), was excessive paternalism on the part of CORA. The other major problem was that of worker incentive. Alongside the collective fields, each family was allocated a private plot; and in order to meet daily expenses, workers were given cash advances on profits from the collective enterprise. These advances, unlike individual wages, were excessively egalitarian, depending as they did on the collective work time of the group, and so they discouraged the responsible worker. Castillo and Lehmann (1983: 252) report that "under the *asentamiento* system, private plots coexisted with and were in effect subsidised by the collective, and the land held collectively remained undercultivated now as on the old *haciendas*, since the incentives to work on one's private plot were far greater." Finally, since the cash advances were perceived as gifts rather than loans, between 1967 and 1970, the default rate on loans was over 33 percent (Chonchol 1977: 202).

It was the intent of the Allende government to "reform the reform"; but with the speed-up in the rate of expropriation and in the short time span before the military coup, these intentions were not accomplished.[9] In spite of the counter-reform, a dramatic change in agrarian structure had occurred. Castillo and Lehmann (1983: 268) point out, "The net result . . . was not a return to the *status quo* but a transformation from a system dominated by huge *haciendas* based on large contingents of tied labour to a system dominated by medium-sized capital-intensive farm units based on wage labour." They add that the medium-sized farms were the most dynamic sector in Chilean agriculture throughout the Frei-Allende period, since they were in a position to benefit from credit and technical assistance and also take advantage of market opportunities.

EMPRESAS ASOCIATIVAS IN PERU

As did Chile, Peru underwent a radical agrarian reform inspired by rising food imports and stagnating production, without a revolution and with landlord compensation. The reform took place under the military government of Juan Velasco Alvarado (1969-80). Cristóbal Kay (1982: 161) says of the reform, "Peru's agrarian reform remains to date one of the boldest experiments of its kind undertaken in Latin America. It effectively destroyed the hitherto existing oligarchical order and created a new institutional framework."

Even as Kay wrote, however, that "new institutional framework" was transforming itself into something again completely new. When Fernando Belaúnde Terry returned to the presidency in 1980, parcellation of the collective farms that had been set up under the Velasco regime began. Michael Carter and Elena Alvarez describe the wildfire spread of the break-up of the Agricultural Producer Cooperatives (CAPs):

> Parcellation has almost completely obliterated the large-farm agriculture, most recently composed of CAPs which heretofore controlled nearly 50 percent of agricultural land. CAP size averaged 710 hectares in these two valleys. Holdings between 3 and 10 hectares now dominate the agrarian structure: this size stratum contains 60 percent of the cultivated area. (Carter and Alvarez 1986: 3)

Whether the parcels will remain in the hands of the small farmer, or be absorbed into a more dynamic medium-sized farm structure as happened in Chile, remains to be seen.

Agrarian reform in Peru began with the Land Reform Bill (15,037) of 1964 under the first Belaúnde presidency (1964-68). Very little land was expropriated, however, before the collectivist reform of the Velasco government.[10] At this time a new reform law was passed creating as a central element *empresas asociativas*—the most common of which was the CAP.[11] Private holdings that were judged to be too large were returned to the workers in the form of an "indivisible production unit in which ownership and usufruct of all productive assets are collective. In theory no individual production is permissible. . . . Profits are only distributed after a series of obligatory deductions for reserve, investment, social security, education and development funds" (Kay 1982: 150).

In the highlands there was intense opposition to the CAPs. The subsistence orientation of the peasant communities was not as conducive to the collective enterprises as was the export-crop agriculture on the coast. It was necessary to allow individual family plots in addition to the collective land. Douglas Horton (1977: 237) reports that "lack of peasant support for group farming has been accompanied by severe managerial problems in highland reform enterprises." He goes on to note that whereas the coastal enterprises could often afford professional managers, those in the highlands had to rely on local talent that was in most cases not up to the job. As in Chile, the individual plots received much more attention than the collective land, whose financial viability, at the time that Horton wrote, was in grave doubt.

The experience on the coast before the parcellation that began in 1981 contrasted with that of the highlands. From an empirical study of 59 CAPs in the central Peruvian coast judging technical efficiency based on input-output data, Michael Carter (1984b: 844) gives the coastal CAPs a mixed review, stating that although some firms were successfully self-managed, "the relatively weak average performance of the CAPs suggests that economically successful labour management is not automatic." Cristóbal Kay, however, questions whether the CAPs could really be considered self-managed enterprises, given the increased level of state intervention. He implies that they might more properly be termed state capitalist (Kay 1982: 157).

With the return of Belaúnde, support for the collectives weakened. Although not activist in promoting parcellation, the new government passed laws such that CAP members could vote to change the organization of their enterprise, and they did so with unanticipated rapidity. Carter and Alvarez attempt to evaluate the transformation to small-scale agriculture with respect to microeconomic factors: "In summary, microeconomic decision-making is being restructured by reform of the Peruvian agrarian reform. Subdivision of CAPs results in changes in incentives, risk-bearing, scale, and market access. From a theoretical point of view, the net effect of these changes on reform sector productivity is ambiguous" (Carter and Alvarez 1986: 14). They stress, however, that the parcellation of the CAPs in Peru occurred very quickly, with little consideration for the potential costs and benefits.

The most positive effect of parcellation on productivity referred to is that of worker incentive. While initial enthusiasm prompted hard work and solidarity of the CAPs to begin with, the "prisoners' dilemma" situation among the workers soon degenerated into a low-effort, low-income result. Carter and Alvarez (1986: 26) state, "Interviewed parceleros report large increases in both hours worked and personal income after parcellation." Due to a very weak statistical base, no conclusive trends in crop yields are forwarded in regard to the pre and post parcellation situation.

The negative effects of this rapid, disorganized decollectivization include the decapitalization of the ex-CAPs, leaving broken-down machinery in "surrealistic graveyards." Loss of production planning, coordinated pest management, and collective marketing are others, along with decreased access to credit and technical assistance. Finally, the small farmer is placed under far greater exposure to risk under parcellation. Carter and Alvarez (1986: 18) question the stability of the current situation, saying that "even if small-scale agriculture per se is statistically viable, medium-sized, capitalized, family farms could emerge through a dynamic survival of the fittest and luckiest."

RECENT REFORMS: EL SALVADOR AND NICARAGUA

Currently in Central America two countries are in the early stages of substantial agrarian reform programs. In Nicaragua the agrarian reform is the outcome of the Sandinista victory, while in El Salvador it came at the urgent prodding of the Carter administration in an attempt to avert "another Nicaragua." Certainly the experience in both countries is very short term and very difficult to assess, especially given the ongoing guerilla warfare in both countries. But it serves to enforce the inescapable fact that land reform is, and will remain, a central political question in Latin America whether or not it can be shown to improve productivity, and it is of interest to note the new directions that agrarian reform programs have taken, given past lessons.

Agrarian reform was initiated in El Salvador in March of 1980 under the government of José Napoleon Duarte. The largest estates were transferred to the former workers and production cooperatives were set up under the direction of the Institute for Agrarian Transformation (ISTA). Landlords are to be compensated over a 30-year period by the cooperatives.

In late 1982, a study team for U.S. AID headed by John Strasma did the field work for what became a fairly positive report (Strasma, Gore, and Nash 1983). Productivity is noted to have held approximately constant to pre-reform levels even given the guerilla warfare. Major problems center around management as they report, "ISTA technicians and promoters are a weak link in the agrarian reform process" (Strasma, Gore, and Nash 1983: 113). The team makes the recommendation that professional managers and accountants be hired where needed and that research be conducted into alternative farming systems. They also report "a refreshing lack of dogmatism about individual farming and production cooperatives; some projects we visited are going one way and some the other" (Strasma, Gore, and Nash 1983: 10). Additionally, surveys were conducted among the members of the cooperatives to get their feelings on cooperative versus individual production. In general, feelings were mixed; and when asked whether the cooperatives should be divided up among members, respondents were split evenly (Strasma, Gore, and Nash 1983: 104-105).

In Nicaragua, after the defeat of Somoza in July of 1979, former Somoza lands and those of his allies were confiscated and organized as state farms managed by the Nicaraguan Institute of Agrarian Reform (INRA). Later in 1982 the emphasis shifted to production cooperatives.

As of 1985, a great diversity of production enterprises were to be found in Nicaragua. Quoting a report by Stanfield and Kaimowitz:

> Today Nicaragua has a wide variety of production enterprises which coexist in a somewhat unique fashion. Private capitalist holdings larger than 350 Hectares still account for 12% of Nicaragua's agricultural land. . . . Small and medium sized private farmers, the majority of whom are organized in credit and service cooperatives, account for 60%. State farms hold 19%, while agricultural production cooperatives make up the difference, with 9%.
>
> Within each of these broad categories a great diversity of form and function can be found. The Nicaraguans have been willing to experiment with new models of production and to modify or even discard them, if they are found to be inappropriate. (Stanfield and Kaimowitz 1985: 2)

Although they commend the flexibility of the Nicaraguan government, the flux in management forms must also be indicative of some need for adjustment. In fact, initial productivity declines and problems of organization are reported on the state farms. As far as the production cooperatives are concerned, however, it is impossible to sort out problems of organization, given that they have been major targets of the counter-revolutionary forces.

OTHER EXAMPLES

As previously demonstrated, almost all countries in Latin America have had at least some degree of agrarian reform, so there is a wealth of experience to add to the question of organizational structure. Certainly all the countries are deserving of much more careful study than will be attempted here. For the sake of an overview, however, brief mention will be made as to the experience of some of the others.

Bolivia

Like that of Mexico and Nicaragua, land reform in Bolivia came as a result of violent revolution. Despite the extent of the reform,[12] its experience with cooperatives and credit programs for the beneficiaries is very limited. After the 1952 revolution, the Land Reform Decree was passed in August of 1953. But the peasants themselves took and independently divided up the former estates. King comments that "the Bolivian land reform seems to be a case of too much too soon and too little afterwards" (King 1977: 118), referring to the chaotic period after the reform and the almost total lack of services such as credit, marketing, and extension. In the five years following the revolution, production dropped by 13 percent and did not regain its 1952 level until 1962 (Furtado 1976: 265). When King wrote in 1977, he reported that "no well-co-ordinated co-operative movement exists for beneficiaries. Complementary services, . . . have largely by-passed the land reform sector and been applied to the commercial development of the Oriente region" (King 1977: 123).

Venezuela

The final major reform to be discussed is the 1960 oil-financed reform of Venezuela. With the democratic revolution of 1945 production cooperatives had been established only to be disintegrated by the military coup of 1948. After land invasions reoccurred in 1958, the Agrarian Reform Law of 1960 was passed to provide land, credit, and technical assistance as basic rights to the beneficiaries. Paul Cox reports, however, that the credit and technical assistance has in general been diverted to the capitalist agricultural sector (Cox 1978). Both individual and collective farming enterprises exist, although more recently the official emphasis has shifted to the collectives with an effort to provide these groups with the necessary services. Cox concludes that "relative to other subsectors of

Venezuelan agriculture, the agrarian reform sector has become less vital
. . . . agrarian reform campesinos are becoming marginalized to the point
of obscurity" (Cox 1978: 55).

Alliance for Progress Reforms

The Charter of Punta del Este was signed in 1961, and between that
time and 1964, thirteen countries enacted agrarian reform legislation
(Grindle 1986: 140). The first of these was Colombia. Hirschman (1963:
155) attributes the enactment of the agrarian reform law principally to
concern over social unrest in the rural areas and to the recognition of low
agricultural productivity. The land reform agency (INCORA) effectively
had the task of expropriating public land to individual farmers, along with
handling irrigation projects and supervised credit. In the *1973 AID Spring
Review of Small Farmer Credit*, Schwinden and Feaster give a rather
positive report of the INCORA supervised credit program with technical
assistance as an effective complement.[13] Surprisingly, Tai gives account of
an abundance of trained technical expertise (Tai 1974: 304). King (1977:
158) reports that due to problems in supervising the loans to small farmers, attention has been shifted to larger farmers.

Some of the other reforms initiated by the Alliance for Progress
include Costa Rica, Ecuador, and Honduras. Although agrarian reform
legislation was enacted in Honduras in 1962, little was done until peasant
organizations invaded public lands in 1967 (Ruhl 1984: 51). In a survey
of 32 agrarian reform settlements with an in-depth study of 4 of those,
Constantina Safilios-Rothschild makes the following conclusion about the
individual, collective, and mixed farming systems:

> Mixed farming systems with half to three-fourths of the land cultivated col-
> lectively and the remainder divided into individual lots represent the best
> types of farming systems, reconciling the advantages of collective farming in
> terms of credit and technical assistance with the peasants' preference for in-
> dividual plots. Asentamientos with no collective farming . . . are not organ-
> ized into cooperatives or precooperatives and, thus, do not have access to
> credit and tend to remain outside ongoing development efforts.[14]

Costa Rica initially attempted colonization of virgin lands, but this
soon turned out to be prohibitively expensive. In a 1979 study Seligson
reports that in the 1970s farms were expropriated in well-developed areas
for communal enterprises during the 1970-74 period and as individual
holdings since 1974. He found individual plots to be highly inefficient due
to lack of capital and also believes that they encouraged larger families for
farm labor, but he comments that the land reform agency was currently
trying to determine whether the communal or individual program was the
more effective (Seligson 1979: 165-66).

Blankstein and Zuvekas (1973) report the generally dismal experience of agrarian reform in Ecuador up to 1970, with almost nothing in
the way of complementary support services. They express much hope for

"a complementary agrarian reform program, the *Programa para Promoción de Empresas Agrícolas*, under which credit and technical assistance are made available to *campesinos* making private land purchases from landowners, to whom payment is assured," and refer to Ecuador as "an important test case for a new approach to agrarian reform in Latin America" (Blankstein and Zuvekas 1973: 94). A Food and Agriculture Organization (FAO) country review paper of 1980, however, reports no improvement with regard to credit and technical assistance; rather, it comments that changing policies and laws has only lead to increased bureaucracy.

The Dominican Republic

The Charter of the Punta del Este for the Dominican Republic practically coincided with the assassination of Rafael Trujillo, who had been dictator for 30 years. In 1962, with the election of Juan Bosch, and with the encouragement of the Alliance for Progress, an agrarian reform law was passed and the Instituto Agrario Dominicano (IAD) was set up to administer the reform. Further legislation, intended to speed-up the distribution, passed in the 1972-74 period, at which time the emphasis also shifted from individual parcels to collective units. The reform has slowly extended itself to benefit 72,509 families, or 19.2 percent of rural households (see Table 1.1), and includes about 14 percent of the agricultural land in the country (Rodríguez-Núñez et al. 1983: 1).

The IAD was given the responsibility of redistributing state and privately owned lands to the rural poor and establishing credit programs and other services such as agricultural extension, marketing, and cooperatives. Lands distributed under the reform program are done so with usufructuary rights and provisional titles only. Parcels may not be sold, although families may inherit rights. Abandoned parcels belong to the state.

In 1983 the Land Tenure Center at the University of Wisconsin, Madison, did a number of case studies of land reform projects in the Dominican Republic in order to come to some conclusion about the appropriate organizational structure. As in most other countries where reforms took place, the projects in the Dominican Republic were set up under a variety of management forms. In some cases individual parcels were allocated to family units, in other cases collective farms were set up, and finally in some cases an intermediate associative model was instituted. David Stanfield and others (1983) emphasize the movement toward the intermediate form of management from both extremes of completely collective and completely individual units.

CONCLUSION

A wealth of experience has accumulated from the variety of organizational structures for land reform projects instituted in Latin America and the evolution of these structures to better suit the needs of the beneficiaries.

Cooperative farming programs offer the opportunity to provide credit to the small farmer under a group plan with lower transaction costs for both the lending institution and the farmer. Other major inputs, such as seed, fertilizer, and capital equipment also yield economies of scale. Additionally, technical assistance can be more easily provided to an organized group of farmers.

However, the problems involved in cooperative farming are not to be overlooked. These problems focus around the internal organization of the project and individual incentive. Divergent goals between members, management, and government agencies cause conflicts of interest. Most importantly, individual members are much less inclined to apply full effort when the reward for that effort is split up evenly among all members.

Disappointment with extremes of complete collectivism and simple individualism have led many to consider mixed alternatives in an effort to capture the benefits of both extremes without all the problems.

In Mexico, where perhaps the most extensive experience with degrees of cooperativism has been gained, most *ejidos* are now farmed individually with centralized credit and marketing. Many studies show a preference for the individual *ejido* over the collective in terms of productivity, and certainly in terms of revealed preference of the beneficiaries, the semi-collective farms have been shown to be superior. The short-lived experience in Chile with private plots for beneficiaries alongside collective land demonstrated that beneficiaries would use the wages of the collective as subsidies for private production and neglect the collective land. The large collective farms set up under the Velasco regime in Peru showed the difficulty of sustaining a collective enterprise under an inadequate administrative structure.

The Dominican Republic provides a further example of a revealed preference by land reform beneficiaries for an intermediate management form. The following chapter introduces the Dominican Republic and the role that agriculture plays in its economy before exploring, in Chapter 3, the agrarian reform projects of the Dominican Republic and the institutions with which they deal.

NOTES

1. Here, no distinction is made between land reform and agrarian reform. Both are defined loosely to refer to any programs, including colonization schemes, that appropriate land to the landless or small farmers.

2. See Barraclough 1971; Carter 1984a; Dorner and Kanel 1977; Tai 1974; Warriner 1969.

3. See, for example, Barraclough 1976; Carroll 1973; Adams and Romero 1981; Tinnermeier 1973.

4. See Stavenhagen 1973: 1-2. Tai ranks this as probably the highest concentration of land in the world at the time (Tai 1974: 26).

5. In FAO, 1980, "Mexico—Country Review Paper" p. 81, it is reported that 83,085 million hectares were distributed to 2,843,837 beneficiaries between 1916 and 1976.

6. See, for example, Stavenhagen 1973 and Eckstein 1971. Stavenhagen concludes that "the ejido as a cooperative enterprise will generally be unable to break the framework of individualism, corruption, private profit-seeking and exploitation which characterize the wider society. . . . The collective ejido in Mexico was born with the sins of the capitalist society upon it" (Stavenhagen 1973: 32-33).

7. According to Tai (1974: 242), 95 percent of the *ejidos* are of the individual type.

8. This generalization is made in Tai 1974: 244.

9. Barraclough (1972: 172), writing soon after the Unidad Popular government came to power, suggests that the Allende regime institute "area cooperatives" that would provide services such as marketing, credit, and technical assistance to member organizations. These member organizations could range from *asentamientos*, post-*asentamientos*, and small holders. He suggests that the "area cooperative" should allow for a highly flexible land tenure system but should charge a rent "for the commercial use of land and capital at their productive values . . . [to] encourage rational use of resources."

10. Tom Alberts reports that of all the land expropriated in the 1962-78 period only 9 percent was from the Belaúnde period, while the remaining 91 percent occurred in the 1969-78 period under Velasco (Alberts 1983: 267).

11. See Horton (1977) for a more complete picture of the various types of enterprises included. Another major form was the SAIS (Agricultural Society of Social Interest), which was set up in the highlands and included, along with the workers of the former estates, neighboring peasants who did not actually work on the estates but shared in the services provided.

12. King (1977: 118) reports that 18 million hectares were distributed to 477,000 beneficiary families.

13. The INCORA credit program began in 1964, made possible by an AID loan of $10 million U.S. and another loan in 1966 of $8.5 million U.S. (Schwinden and Feaster 1973: iv).

14. The focus of the study, however, is on the role of women in the agrarian reform (Safilios-Rothschild 1983: 18).

2

The Dominican Republic as a Case Study

The Dominican Republic, although isolated in the Caribbean from its counterparts in Latin America, in many ways typifies the countries in Latin America. Wiarda and Kryzanek emphasize its role as a microcosm and a bellwether of the Latin American experience:

> Within this small nation's borders and throughout its history it is possible to see all the wrenching divisions, developmental dilemmas, crises, and controversies characteristic of Latin America. . . . [It] has frequently provided a fascinating preview of important shifts in the directions of Latin American political change and of U.S. policy toward the area. . . . For a time the Dominican Republic was the showcase for the ill-fated American aid program known as the Alliance for Progress. (Wiarda and Kryzanek 1982: 1-2)

With respect to agrarian reform, the experience of the Dominican Republic is also typical of that in the rest of Latin America. Its *latifundio-minifundio* landholding structure, early colonization efforts with foreign immigrants, agrarian reform under the Alliance for Progress, and continuing experiments with collectively and individually farmed land reform projects bring together many of the essential elements of the agrarian reform experience in Latin America. For this reason it has been chosen as the case in point for this study.

In this chapter, the political and economic history of the Dominican Republic is briefly overviewed. Then, the history of land settlement is covered, followed by a review of the current role of agriculture in the Dominican economy.

THE SPANISH LEGACY

The Early Years

Founded in 1493 as the first colony of Spain in the New World, Santo Domingo, as it was then called, was initially very important to the rising Spanish empire as an administrative seat and strategically located port. The island was first exploited for its gold, and the native population was put to work in the mines. The gold did not last long, however; nor did the native Indians. Frank Moya Pons in his *Manual de Historia Dominicana* reports that "in 1519 they were scarcely able to obtain some 2,000 pesos of gold in the mines and that signified the extinction of the gold economy conjunctly with the extinction of the native arms that made possible its development"[1] (Moya Pons 1978: 29).

Sugar replaced gold in the colonial economy and the Indians were replaced by slaves from Africa. According to Moya Pons, by 1527 there were already 25 sugar factories (Moya Pons 1978: 32). Initially prosperous, the island was to undergo many years of turmoil and stagnation. With the conquest of Mexico the golden era of the colony of Hispaniola came to an end. Wiarda and Kryzanek describe the depressed state of the island as Spain became distracted with her other larger colonies on the mainland:

> Hispaniola became an underpopulated, undeveloped, and forgotten colony that offered little to the mother country or even to passing pirates. Its once-flourishing mines and plantations were abandoned, the economy reverted to a more primitive subsistence state, and the city of Santo Domingo fell into a bedraggled condition. What trade existed was primarily in cowhides, for the staple commodities like sugar, cotton and tobacco that would later make the economy grow again were not properly managed or developed. The island was socially, politically, and economically disorganized and unorganized. (Wiarda and Kryzanek 1982: 26)

Turmoil and Stagnation

The colony remained in this depressed state for over two hundred years as it became the battlefield for struggles among the European powers. England attacked the island and later, in 1655, the French gained control of the western coasts, which were to become Haiti. In the second half of the eighteenth century trade opened up and population increased dramatically, a large portion of which consisted of slaves from Africa. Toussaint L'Ouverture led a revolt in the French colony, freed the slaves, invaded the Spanish colony to the east, and united the island in January 1801 under his own leadership. The Spanish elite were horrified and fled, taking with them wealth, cultural tradition, and education. Napoleon Bonaparte, in power in France, sent troops to Santo Domingo in 1802, and the Dominicans joined them to push the Haitians back to the west.

In 1809 the colony was returned to Spanish rule. Slavery was reimposed, and some of the former aristocracy returned. Economic conditions did not improve, however, and between 1822 and 1844 Santo Domingo was again under Haitian rule. The tyranny of the reign paralyzed the economy, agriculture was neglected, the large estates were in ruin, and generally chaos prevailed.

Independence and U.S. Occupation

Independence came on February 27, 1844, due to the efforts of Los Trinitarios, a nationalistic secret society under the direction of Juan Pablo Duarte. But with independence came power struggles, dictatorships, and civil wars that prevailed until 1916 when, with Europe at war, the United States stepped in to occupy the country, an occupation that lasted through 1924. This was not the first intervention in Dominican sovereignty by the United States, however. Already, at the turn of the century, the U.S. government had taken over the collection of Dominican customs duties to collect unpaid debt.

Under the U.S. occupation, or the Gobierno Militar as it was called by the Dominicans, some degree of order was established. World War I brought on the rise in prices of primary products, especially sugar, tobacco, cocoa, and coffee. Economic prosperity was restored, but at the expense of the consolidation of small agriculture, which had developed during the years of turmoil and stagnation, into sugar plantations under foreign investment. Moya Pons reports that

> as their plantations grew, more and more lands fell under their dominion while many communities that before carried out an agricultural or pastoral existence independently, disappeared. At the end of the Occupation, the sugar industry controlled more that 2 million *tareas* [approximately 125,000 hectares], of agricultural land, which was an exorbitant quantity.[2] (Moya Pons 1978: 494)

The Rise of Trujillo

Although the United States withdrew its forces in 1924, the military framework prevailed. Under the presidency of Horacio Vásquez, Rafael Trujillo, a leader of the Policía Nacional Dominicana under the occupation, consolidated his power in the new Ejército Nacional and in 1930 instituted himself as president of the Dominican Republic. The dictatorship, which was to last 31 years, despite its tyranny brought stability and with it economic growth. Public works were initiated and highways expanded. Trujillo, however, used his power for his own personal benefit and obtained a very large monopoly on the sugar and other export industries. This exploitation of the rest of the economy for the good of the Trujillo family enterprises caused distortions of the rural economy that have been very difficult to correct.

Post Trujillo

Trujillo was assassinated in May of 1961, and in 1962 Juan Bosch, a moderate leftist, was elected president and promoted land reform as the core of his economic program. But within seven months he lost power to a military coup. Then in 1965 the United States intervened and in 1966 Joaquín Balaguer, who had served under Trujillo, was elected president. His 12-year administration was followed by the reign of the Partida Reformista Dominicana—first under the presidency of Antonio Guzmán and then under Jorge Blanco. More recently, in May of 1986, the presidency was returned to the ageing Balaguer.

THE LAND AND LAND SETTLEMENT

The Land Base

Of the many problems the Dominican Republic has had to deal with in its efforts to improve the productive potential of its share of the island of Hispaniola, an unfavorable land base is not one of them. In contrast to Haiti, which covers the western third of the island, with dry rugged terrain and denuded mountain slopes, in the Dominican Republic the land is fertile, the climate is temperate, and rainfall is moderate.

The land area of 19,386 square miles,[3] covering the eastern two-thirds of the island of Hispaniola, is cut by four east-west mountain ranges. In the north-central area lies the "food basket"—the largest and most fertile valley—the Cibao. Most of the food for domestic consumption—rice, corn, beans, and cattle—is produced here as well as substantial exports in cocoa, bananas, tobacco, and coffee. South of the next mountain range is the San Juan Valley, which is also quite fertile and produces peanuts, cotton, rice, and yuca. The southernmost valley, the Neiba, produces sugar and rice. The coastal plains in the eastern sector of the island were, for almost 20 years prior to 1985, owned almost entirely by Gulf and Western Corporation.[4] This area has the most productive sugar lands—sugar being the major export of the country[5]—as well as many fine pasturelands for cattle. Most of the country receives adequate rainfall, and an expanding irrigation network from the country's three major rivers allows farming in otherwise arid regions.

Colonial Land Settlement

The fertile valleys and lush flora and fauna impressed Christopher Columbus when he first landed on the island in 1493. Under instructions from the Spanish Crown, he began to distribute land to the Spaniards under a system known as *repartimiento*. The assignments of land were accompanied by Indians to work the land. Marlin Clausner explains that the Indians had legal status as "free vassals" (as of 1500), were not slaves, but could be forced to work. He comments, "This consideration was a practical one. At the turn of the century, the Spaniards in Espaola, as later elsewhere in the New World, could not afford to treat the Indians as equals in all respects. If not the Indians, who would perform the labor?" (Clausner 1973: 24).

Figure 2.1
Relief Features of Hispaniola

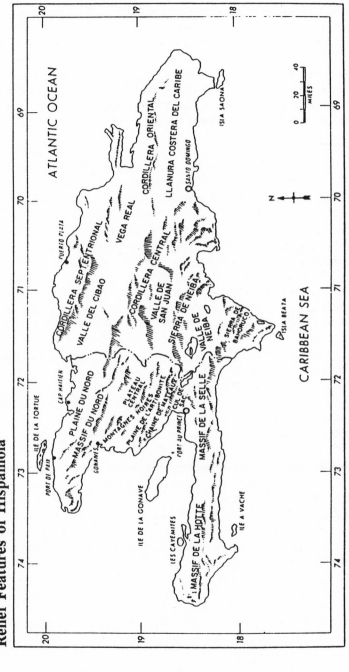

Source: Black, Jan Knippers, *The Dominican Republic: Politics and Development in an Unsovereign State* (Boston, MA.: Allen & Unwin, 1986), page 5, Relief Features of Hispaniola. Illustration copyright 1986 by Allen & Unwin, Inc. Reprinted with permission.

The Instructions of 1503 substituted the *repartimiento* system with a more formal *encomienda* system in which each family was given an individual plot for their own subsistence. The *encomenderos* were not to abuse the Indians, who were in theory under the protection of the Crown, but were granted their services. Effectively, however, "the practice of encomienda [was] . . . the equivalent of little more than uncompensated slavery" (Clausner 1973: 37). By 1513, for purposes of promoting interests of the Church, the Crown began to shift from individual to communal land tenure for the Indians (Clausner 1973: 36-38).

The Slave State

At this time the Indian population was declining rapidly. Slave importation had begun in 1503, and by 1520 virtually all labor was provided by the black slaves from Africa. Notwithstanding, the population of the island dropped dramatically. As Spaniards left in search of greater treasures on the mainland, many farms were abandoned. Those Spaniards who remained seized more and more land, most governing it in absentia, such that agriculture was sorely neglected (Black 1986: 16-17).

In the second half of the eighteenth century with the increase in trade, the restrictions on slave trade were removed and the slave population increased dramatically, prior to the rebellion led by Toussaint L'Ouverture. Clausner reports the effect on land tenure of the takeover by L'Ouverture:

> Toussaint's rule over Santo Domingo was brief, but in a period of about a year and a half he issued a number of decrees, two of which were to affect the ownership of land in Santo Domingo for generations. He abolished slavery and ordered all property of Spaniards in exile to be confiscated and turned over to his government. These two actions brought agricultural activity to a standstill and upset the traditional norms of ownership. Land records were lost or destroyed during the confiscatory process as the old Spanish colonial administrative structure was dismantled. (Clausner 1973: 75-76)

During the colonial era communal land had been allocated to Spanish settlements, but boundaries between state lands and rural communal lands were not clearly defined. Under Haitian rule these lands were divided up; but when independence came, in 1845, the Haitian orders were reversed. Later, in 1911, legislation was introduced to partition communal land. Clausner reports, however, that neither the 1845 nor the 1911 laws were heeded (Clausner 1973: 125-26).

Land Registration under the U.S. Occupation

Under the U.S. occupation, the land registration law was passed in 1920 and the Torrens system[6] of land title registration was instituted. Although it cleared up the confusion in land-ownership, the law also called for the partition of communal land. In the process, Black explains, "communal landholders and squatters without titles were displaced in large numbers as sugar companies and other commercial plantations added thousands upon thousands of acres to their properties. Even peasants who owned individual family plots were no match for corporations that could hire gaggles of lawyers" (Black 1986: 23).

Consolidation under Trujillo

The Trujillo regime, which lasted over 30 years, had major ramifications for land tenure. Trujillo consolidated not only power and wealth but also land on a grand scale. Ian Bell describes the extent of Trujillo's appetite for land:

> Some of the land he acquired was virgin and some of it was pastoral; and much of it he turned into sugar plantations. Trujillo's methods of acquiring the land ranged from purchase at a knockdown price by intimidation or blackmail to outright confiscation. His appetite for good land, whether pastoral or arable, was such that many hitherto successful farmers deliberately ran their farms down so as not to attract his covetous attention. (Bell 1981: 281)

It is estimated that the Trujillo family owned about one-third of all cultivable land, half the sugar industry, and almost all other agricultural exports (Weil 1973: 44), controlling up to 60 percent of the labor force as well as the economic assets of the country (Wiarda and Kryzanek 1982: 36).

At the death of Trujillo, the lands of the Trujillo family were passed to the state. Those lands devoted to cane were placed under the control of the State Sugar Council, and agrarian reform was initiated.

AGRICULTURE CURRENTLY IN THE DOMINICAN REPUBLIC

The Contribution of Agriculture to the Dominican Economy

The leading sector in the economy until the mid-1970s, agriculture has been surpassed by industry in percentage composition of gross domestic product. In 1986 agriculture contributed 16.2 percent to GDP, down from 30 percent in the early 1960s. Mining, construction, and services have increased to pick up the slack. Preliminary results of the 1981 population census noted the economically active population employed in agriculture at only 23.6 percent, (*R.D. en Cifras 1986*: 284) down from almost 60 percent in 1965 (*World Development Report 1987*: 264). The high growth rates of GDP experienced in the early 1970s have slowed almost to a halt in the 1984-86 period, while GDP from agriculture decreased by close to 8 percent from 1983 to 1986. (See Tables 2.1 and 2.2.)

Much of this recent decrease in agricultural production is due to a reduction by the United States of import quotas on sugar entering from the Dominican Republic and by a fall in sugar prices. Sugar has long been the principal export crop of the Dominican Republic (see Table 2.5),

Table 2.1
Percentage Composition of GDP by Sector

	1950–52	1960–62	1966–68	1973–75	1981–83	1984–86[a]
Agriculture	28.6	30.0	25.1	19.4	17.2	16.7
Crops	21.3	21.6	16.4	12.6	10.4	9.8
Livestock	6.8	7.5	7.9	6.3	6.1	6.1
Forestry	0.5	0.9	0.8	0.5	0.7	0.7
Mining	0.2	1.5	1.4	5.6	3.7	4.1
Industry	15.3	15.5	15.0	17.1	18.3	17.0
Construction	4.5	2.8	4.4	7.1	6.5	6.3
Housing	7.2	6.8	7.9	7.5	6.5	6.7
Commerce	18.6	17.4	17.0	18.1	15.2	15.7
Trans, Communic	4.7	5.8	7.5	8.0	9.9	9.9
Finance	1.1	1.6	1.7	1.7	2.5	3.3
Government	9.0	10.7	11.7	6.3	10.0	10.5
Other Services	10.9	7.8	8.4	9.3	8.9	9.7

[a]Figures are preliminary.
Sources: 1950–75 from Graber, 1978, p. 23; 1981–86 from SEA, *Plan Operativa,
1987*, p. 177.

Table 2.2
Share of Agriculture in GDP (millions of 1970 DR$)

	GDP	GDP from Ag	Share of Ag in GDP	Growth Rates GDP	GDP from Ag
1950–52			28.6%		
1960–62			30.0%		
1966–68			25.1%		
1975	2288.9	399.9	17.5%		
1976	2442.9	429.1	17.6%	6.7%	7.3%
1977	2564.4	436.7	17.0%	5.0%	1.8%
1978	2619.5	456.8	17.4%	2.1%	4.6%
1979	2738.2	461.7	16.9%	4.5%	1.1%
1980	2904.9	484.2	16.7%	6.1%	4.9%
1981	3021.9	510.8	16.9%	4.0%	5.5%
1982	3072.5	534.3	17.4%	1.7%	4.6%
1983	3193.6	550.2	17.2%	3.9%	3.0%
1984[a]	3205.5	549.0	17.1%	0.4%	-0.2%
1985[a]	3131.3	524.4	16.7%	-2.3%	-4.5%
1986[b]	3151.8	510.6	16.2%	0.7%	-2.6%

[a]Preliminary
[b]Projections
Sources: 1950–68 from Graber, 1978, p. 23; 1975–86 from SEA, *Plan Operativa,
1987*, p. 176.

accounting for over half of export earnings until quite recently; and the
United States is its principal trading partner—in 1985, 68.9 percent of
Dominican exports were destined to the United States. The value of sugar

exports in 1986 (in 1973 DR$) was less than half that of 1973 and 1974 (see Table 2.4). Agricultural exports, however, although declining in importance, still account for more than 50 percent of total exports (see Table 2.5).

Other traditional export crops are coffee, cocoa, and tobacco. In 1985, together they made up 18.9 percent of total exports (see Table 2.3). Growth in agricultural exports has occurred since 1980 in cocoa, as well as roots crops (see Table 2.4).

Table 2.3
Principal Export Commodities as Percentage of Total Exports (millions US$)

	1955	1960	1965	1970	1975	1980	1985
Sugar	58.6	49.6	55.8	51.8	64.5	32.2	25.8
Coffee	15.6	12.6	15.3	13.5	4.8	7.9	7.8
Cocoa					3.2	5.8	8.8
Tobacco					3.8	3.6	2.3
Ferronickel						10.5	16.4
Dore						26.9	15.4
Bauxite					1.8	1.9	

Source: *Statistical Abstract of Latin America*, Vol. 25, Tables 2400–2403.

Table 2.4
Value of Principal Agricultural Exports, 1973–86 (millions of 1973 DR$)

	Sugar	Coffee	Cocoa	Tobacco	Beef	Guandul	Tubers[b]
1973	154.9	40.0	19.5	29.5	3.8	3.1	2.9
1974	157.7	34.5	22.3	38.8	7.4	3.4	2.8
1975	144.4	28.2	18.8	29.6	3.3	3.7	1.8
1976	140.4	41.3	20.6	31.1	8.4	3.3	3.2
1977	164.8	45.0	21.7	18.6	1.2	2.9	3.0
1978	142.8	51.1	23.2	20.1	1.5	3.5	3.8
1979	148.4	44.5	21.3	38.8	1.8	0.4	3.1
1980	118.3	29.0	19.5	20.7	1.8	3.3	3.1
1981	126.9	30.8	22.9	37.8	5.3	3.2	4.3
1982	123.6	39.2	32.2	11.6	5.7	3.7	4.0
1983	137.0	33.1	29.0	12.7	4.3	5.6	4.5
1984	124.3	32.6	25.1	16.3	0.6	5.3	4.7
1985	99.5	37.9	26.4	13.6	10.0	4.4	8.2
1986[a]	75.1	31.6	30.4	11.7	9.2	1.6	5.5

[a]1986 figures are preliminary.
[b]Tubers include yautia, yuca, ñame, yams.

Source: SEA, *Plan Operativa, 1987*, p. 204.

Table 2.5
Agricultural Exports as Percentage of Total Exports

	Agricultural Exports	Total Exports	Ag Exports as % Total
	(millions US$)		
1982	477.7	767.7	62.2%
1983	456.8	785.2	58.2%
1984	496.2	868.1	57.2%
1985	371.7	738.5	50.3%
1986	392.7	722.1	54.4%

Source: Banco Central de la República Dominicana, *Boletín Mensual*, January 1987, p. 102.

Rice is by far the most important cash crop following sugar cane, but production generally falls short of domestic demand. In only four years since 1973 has it not been necessary to import rice. Plantain and red beans[7] are also major crops in the Dominican Republic; while plantain is not imported, red beans in general are. Although the Dominican Republic was self-sufficient in both rice and beans from 1982 through 1984, there were renewed imports in 1985 due to high input prices and lack of credit availability. Other major agricultural imports include corn, wheat, and oil (see Tables 2.6 and 2.7).

Table 2.6
Value of Production of Principal Agricultural Products, 1983

	Production 000 qqs	Value 000 DR$
Rice	7109	184.8
Cocoa	931	63.4
Plantain	604	54.4
Red Beans	958	38.3
Tobacco	419	21.0
Coffee	700	19.3
Garlic	136	17.5
Yuca	2040	16.3
Peanuts	728	14.6
Tomato-Industrial	2703	8.9
Yautia	584	8.8
Sorghum	849	7.9
Corn	848	7.4
Guandul	285	4.9
Yams	707	4.9
Potatoes	389	4.6
Black Beans*	128	3.7
Red Onion	296	3.6
Name	173	2.1
Tomato-Salad	206	2.1
Squash	128	1.3

*Value is calculated with 1982 price.
Notes: Sugar cane is not included.
        1 qq = 100 lbs.
Source: SEA, *Plan Operativa, 1987*, p. 181.

Table 2.7
Value of Principal Agricultural Imports, 1973–86 (millions of 1973 DR$)

	Rice	Red Bean	Corn	Wheat	Oil
1973	13.7	5.6	6.8	7.9	13.8
1974	32.5	1.0	8.4	3.5	17.1
1975	22.9	2.8	4.7	1.9	14.1
1976	14.8	2.8	7.5	4.2	20.9
1977	29.8	1.9	9.4	6.8	17.5
1978	4.9	1.4	13.2	3.1	19.5
1979		3.3	9.3	11.2	15.7
1980	18.8	3.4	19.4		23.4
1981	29.1		19.0		25.8
1982			19.8		24.6
1983			26.7		27.1
1984			22.8	28.7	25.9
1985	10.2	4.7	32.9	23.4	33.6
1986a	55.0	2.5	34.2	22.2	34.5

a1986 figures are preliminary.
Source: SEA, *Plan Operativa, 1987*, p. 204.

The Modernization of Dominican Agriculture

Although major increases of productivity have occurred in rice, the major export crops, along with beans, show deterioration in yield per hectare since the early 1960s and even the 1950s, as demonstrated in Table 2.8.

Table 2.8
Productivity of Major Agricultural Crops in the Dominican Republic (100kg/ha)

	Sugar	Rice	Cocoa	Beans	Tobacco	Coffee
1981–84	623.2	36.8	3.4	8.8	12.4	3.9
1961–65	694.0		4.5			
1948–52		14.8		8.9	11.0	3.6

Source: Calculated from *Statistical Abstract of Latin America*, Vol. 25, Tables 2104–2116; *Statistical Abstract of Latin America*, Vol. 23, Tables 1503–1515.

Particularly in the major export crops, (sugar, cocoa, tobacco, and coffee) the Dominican Republic ranks low in productivity per hectare among Latin American countries (see Table 2.9). Although falling above all but 3 and 4 of 20 Latin American countries for productivity of rice and beans respectively, in sugar productivity the Dominican Republic ranks ninth among 19; in cocoa it ranks eleventh among 16; in tobacco it ranks fifteenth among 20; and in coffee it ranks thirteenth among 17.

Table 2.9
Productivity of Major Agricultural Crops, 1981–84 Average
(100 kg/ha)

	Sugar	Rice	Cocoa	Beans	Tobacco	Coffee
Dom Rep	623.2	36.8	3.4	8.8	12.4	3.9
Argentina	481.6	37.0		10.9	12.1	
Bolivia	410.5	15.4	5.5	10.6	9.9	8.6
Brazil	600.2	15.4	6.4	4.6	13.2	6.5
Chile		35.9		11.5	29.0	
Colombia	861.5	45.1	5.3	7.1	15.6	8.0
Costa Rica	487.0	22.8	3.0	4.6	12.4	14.1
Cuba	536.4	34.9	7.4	7.6	6.4	4.6
Ecuador	664.1	30.1	2.7	5.6	17.8	2.8
El Salvador	704.3	35.6	9.7	7.6	17.4	8.8
Guatemala	731.0	29.0	5.0	8.5	18.4	6.1
Haiti	375.0	20.5	19.3	5.5	10.0	10.9
Honduras	332.8	19.9	10.0	6.0	10.9	6.4
Mexico	667.4	32.7	4.8	6.4	15.4	5.4
Nicaragua	674.2	34.6	1.5	7.0	18.7	5.6
Panama	516.0	18.8	2.7	3.8	15.3	3.2
Paraguay	400.8	20.9		7.6	13.0	10.1
Peru	1305.1	45.2	5.8	8.9	12.7	6.5
Uruguay	511.0	50.5		6.0	16.9	
Venezuela	595.5	27.0	2.1	5.3	15.9	2.4
U.S.	863.1	53.5		15.9	23.3	10.0

Source: Calculated from *Statistical Abstract of Latin America*, Vol. 25, Tables
2104–2116.

The poor productivity of Dominican agriculture may be associated
with the low adoption of the use of modern inputs, demonstrated in Table
2.10.

In terms of tractors in use per hectare of arable land, for 1982 only
five countries in Latin America show a lower rate of mechanization. In
fertilizer consumption, the Dominican Republic ranks near the middle of
the 21 countries listed in Table 2.10. In terms of irrigated land, however,
the percentage of arable land that is irrigated in the Dominican Republic
exceeds that of most countries in Latin America. In 1982 it registered 16
percent as compared to an average of 10 percent in Latin America. By
1986 that figure had increased to over 20 percent.[8]

Table 2.10
Fertilizer Consumption, Tractors in Use, and Irrigated Land, 1982

	Fertilizer Consumption (H G / Ha)	Tractors In Use (N / 100)	Irrigated Land as % Total	Arable Land (T Ha)
Dom Rep	353	0.295	16.0%	1100
Argentina	31	0.592	6.2%	26000
Bolivia	8	0.023	4.6%	3250
Brazil	365	0.548	3.2%	63000
Chile	189	0.651	23.6%	5330
Colombia	538	0.706	7.9%	4050
Costa Rica	1134	2.138	9.2%	283
Cuba	1726	2.547	39.4%	2540
Ecuador	277	0.409	30.1%	1760
El Salvador	830	0.596	19.6%	560
Guatemala	498	0.311	5.5%	1300
Haiti	51	0.098	12.7%	550
Honduras	137	0.210	5.4%	1570
Mexico	778	0.721	23.7%	21900
Nicaragua	186	0.212	7.6%	1085
Panama	469	0.887	6.1%	462
Paraguay	39	0.207	3.8%	1640
Peru	266	0.456	36.9%	3200
Uruguay	376	2.391	6.3%	1403
Venezuela	408	1.299	10.3%	3080
U. S.	867	2.437	10.9%	188755
Latin America		0.633	10.0%	144063
World	779			

Source: *Statistical Abstract of Latin America*, Vol. 25, Tables 200, 204, 210, 211.

These global comparisons, however, are not entirely adequate as measures of degrees of relative modernization. Certainly fertilizer consumption, mechanization, and irrigation necessarily depend to a great extent on the specific crops grown. More would be learned by comparing techniques in each individual crop. In the Dominican Republic in the mid-1950s, 80 percent of all fertilizer consumed was for sugar cane and rice.[9]

Concentration of Land and Rural Poverty

The concentration of land that occurred under Trujillo, has not been significantly altered by subsequent agrarian reform. Table 2.11 reveals the distribution of farmland by size of farm, recorded in the 1950, 1971, and 1981 agricultural censuses.

In 1981, as in 1950, the largest 0.8 percent of farms covered about 45 percent of the total area in farms, while farms under 10 hectares comprised around 90 percent of the total number and little more than 20 percent of the total area.

Table 2.11
Distribution of Farmland by Size of Farm, 1950, 1971, 1981

	Number of Farms		Area of Farms	
	(Thous)	as % of Total	(Thous H)	as % of Total
1950				
Less than 1 H	92.9	33.8%	47.9	2.1%
1 to 5 H	116.6	42.4%	270.4	11.6%
5 to 10 H	32.9	12.0%	224.7	9.7%
10 to 50 H	27.0	9.8%	543.6	23.3%
50 to 100 H	3.2	1.2%	223.5	9.6%
100 to 500 H	1.8	0.7%	344.4	14.8%
500 H and over	0.3	0.1%	673.7	28.9%
Total	274.7	100.0%	2328.2	100.0%
1971				
Less than .5 H	49.7	16.3%	12.2	0.4%
.5 to 5 H	185.3	60.8%	339.6	12.4%
5 to 10 H	33.8	11.1%	231.4	8.5%
10 to 50 H	29.0	9.5%	587.8	21.5%
50 to 100 H	4.0	1.3%	268.5	9.8%
100 to 500 H	2.7	0.9%	516.8	18.9%
500 H and over	0.4	0.1%	780.0	28.5%
Total	304.8	100.0%	2736.4	100.0%
1981				
Less than .5 H	61.7	16.0%	12.5	0.5%
.5 to 5 H	253.0	65.7%	313.6	11.7%
5 to 10 H	32.5	8.5%	231.8	8.7%
10 to 50 H	30.8	8.0%	640.5	23.9%
50 to 100 H	4.1	1.1%	271.9	10.2%
100 to 500 H	2.6	0.7%	482.8	18.0%
500 H and over	0.3	0.1%	723.5	27.0%
Total	385.1	100.0%	2676.7	100.0%

Sources: *Cuarto Censo Nacional Agropecuario 1950*, R.D.; *R.D. en Cifras, 1986*,
   p. 75.

It should be noted that agrarian reform parcels average 3 hectares and that it is impossible to tell from the tables if there are more farms of this size, in 1981, relative to farms less than half this size. Additionally, much of the agrarian reform land was appropriated as collective farms and consequently the redistributional effects would not be visible here.

Policy and Politics in Agriculture

Currently agricultural policy is focused on diversification of agriculture away from sugar to nontraditional crops including citrus, tomato, African palm, and other fruits and vegetables. Particularly, U.S. AID has encouraged this effort and provided support to the tune of 142 million DR$ in a package announced in August of 1986.

President Balaguer, on the other hand, declared agrarian reform to be the "novia" (bride) of his government, in a speech in July of 1987 (Listín Diario, July 12, 1987). This speech was only one of many, as Balaguer has made weekly weekend expeditions to the country.

Other priorities in agriculture are the move to self-sufficiency in rice and beans, increased credit for the modernization of agriculture, and renovation of the coffee and cocoa fields.

CONCLUSION

The political and economic history of the Dominican Republic is not unlike that for the rest of Latin America. Inequality of land distribution in the Dominican Republic can be traced to its colonial roots, and the development of the fertile land base of Santo Domingo into productive agriculture was continually arrested by political turbulence. Under the dictatorship of Trujillo, consolidation of the productive land occurred on a grand scale—and its repercussions have yet to be alleviated. More recently the Dominican Republic has faced the consequences of the fall of the sugar industry, which has been, for too many years, the mainstay of the Dominican economy.

NOTES

1. "En 1519 apenas se pudieron obtener unos 2,000 pesos de oro en las minas y eso significaba la extinción de la economía aurífera conjuntamente con la extinción de los brazos nativos que hicieron posible su desarrollo." This and all other translations of quotations in Spanish are mine.

2. "A medida que sus plantaciones fueron creciendo, más y más tierras quedaron bajo su dominio desapareciendo muchas comunidades rurales que antes llevaban una vida agrícola o ganadera independiente. Al terminar la Ocupacíon, la industria azucarera controlaba más de 2 millones de tareas de tierra agrícola, que era una cantidad exorbitante."

3. This area is equal to 4.838 million hectares of which 1.4 million hectares is cropland and 2.1 million hectares is pasture (E.I.U. 1986b: 9).

4. Jan Knippers Black documents the transfer of the land and other assets to some Florida-based agribusiness firms (Black 1986: 68-69).

5. Until the last ten years sugar produced over half of export earnings (see Table 2.3).

6. As explained by Clausner (1973: 200), under the Torrens system, "all land purchases would be considered as having been made directly from the state. Legally the title would appear to have been transferred from the old owner to the state and from the state to the new owner. The legal actions, with respect to transfer of property, required that the property first be identified accurately and given exclusive and complete regis-

tration in one official registry book; that title to the property be examined carefully prior to registration to insure its clarity and legality; that all possibly interested third parties be publicly advised of the proposed transfer; and, finally, that a legally competent official transfer to the buyer in good faith a legal and official property title."

7. Rice, beans, and plantain provide the basis of the Dominican diet.

8. SEA, *Plan Operativa 1987*: 197, and *Statistical Abstract of Latin America*, Vol. 25, Table 200.

9. *Estudio de Base del Sector Agropecuario y Forestal*, Secretariado Técnico de la Presidencia, August, 1982, p. 152.

3

Agrarian Reform in the Dominican Republic

The first real efforts toward land reform in the Dominican Republic, like most countries in Latin America, followed the Cuban revolution. In the case of the Dominican Republic, however, the death of Trujillo in 1961 provided further rational for a restructuring of the country's landed assets. The first agrarian reform law was passed in June of 1962, and the Instituto Agrario Dominicano was established to administer the reform program. Further legislation, intended to speed-up the distribution, passed in the 1972–74 period, and at this time there was a shift in emphasis from individual parcels to collective units. More recently in March of 1985, Law No. 269 was passed legalizing a semi-collective form of organization called the *asociativo*. Under this structure, beneficiaries are each responsible for their own plot of land but organize to obtain group credit and realize whatever other collective activities the association decides appropriate. This law was primarily in response to demands by collective farms to alter the collective structure, but it was also intended to encourage the formation of *asociativos* by those beneficiaries who had been assigned individual rights.

This chapter reviews the experience of agrarian reform in the Dominican Republic, focusing on the organizational structure of the reform projects. First discussed is the early experience with land settlement programs preceding the agrarian reform period. Then the institutional framework of the reform sector is considered. The chapter

An article based upon material drawn from this chapter appears in the August 1989 issue of *World Development*, published by Pergamon Journals Ltd., Oxford, England.

continues with an exploration of the active role the agrarian reform sector has come to play in rice production in the Dominican Republic, especially under the collective form of production. The recent movement toward the intermediate associative management form is introduced and efforts to evaluate the collective and individual forms are surveyed. Finally, the chapter focuses specifically on the organization of the projects themselves, referring to particular cases in the northwest involved in a transformation from both extremes of individual and collective management to the intermediate associative form.

EARLY COLONIZATION

Prior to the agrarian reform law of 1962, the extent of land redistribution in the Dominican Republic consisted of the colonization projects initiated under the Trujillo dictatorship. Not properly a land reform program, the colonies were an attempt to settle scarcely populated areas with landless *campesinos* and foreign immigrants. The Agricultural Colonization Law passed in 1927 gave them the right to settle specific plots of land; and if they complied with conditions of the law, they were, after a five-year period, granted title to the holding. A U.S. Department of Agriculture source reports the following: "In 1940 of the 218,060 farms included in the census, 15,942 were operated by colonists. According to the 1950 census only 4,390 farms were being operated by colonists. Large numbers of colonists acquired titles to property during this period and were not classified as colonists in the 1950 census" (U.S. Department of Agriculture 1961: 2).

Table 3.1 demonstrates the extent of the colonization in relation to the later reform programs.

Table 3.1
Agrarian Reform in the Dominican Republic up to 1986: Type of Projects, Families Benefitted, and Land Distributed

Type of Projects	Number	%	Families Benefitted	%	Land Distributed (in hectares)	%
Colonies 1927–61	40	6.9	11,451	15.8	140,797	34.9
Individ. 1962–86	278	47.8	33,013	45.5	171,991	42.7
Collect./ Assoc. 1973–86	263	45.3	28,045	38.7	90,360	22.4
Total	581	100.0	72,509	100.0	403,149	100.0

Source: IAD, *Boletín Informativo Anual, 1986.*

John P. Augelli (1962) gives a rather glowing report of the colonization in the Dominican Republic and describes its success in attracting foreign immigrants, including Jewish refugees settling in Sosua along with Hungarians, Spaniards, and other Europeans in the central mountains in Constanza and Jarabacoa. There were also a great many Japanese, who were among the most successful of the colonists. Essentially, the bulk of the colonies were set up along the Haitian border for protection. The U.S. Department of Agriculture disagrees with Augelli's report of much government support and says that "generally they [the colonies] were not successful because of lack of planning, credit, and technical assistance" (Mears 1963: 9).

POST-1961 REFORMS: THE INSTITUTIONAL FRAME-WORK

The assassination of Trujillo in 1961, along with encouragement from the conference at Punta del Este in the same year, provided the impetus for agrarian reform in the Dominican Republic. The Trujillo lands were confiscated by the state, and the State Sugar Council (CEA) was established to manage his former estates. Other lands were invaded by squatters, and those who had lost lands to the former dictator reasserted their rights.

The 1962 Law and the Instituto Agrario Dominicano

The Agrarian Reform Law 5879 was passed on June 14, 1962, just prior to the election of Juan Bosch, who campaigned with a platform based on agrarian reform. The law established the IAD (Instituto Agrario Dominicano) to administer the reform program giving it the responsibility to redistribute state and privately owned lands to the rural poor. Among the other activities to be undertaken by the IAD were the establishment of irrigation projects, credit programs, and other services such as agricultural extension, marketing, and cooperatives, as well as the inventory and titling of state lands.

The legal status of the IAD is described by Joseph R. Thome, in an early report to U.S. AID on the progress of the reform, as follows:

> The IAD is a semi-autonomous agency with the power to contract its own financial obligations, subject to the approval of the Executive Power. It is supposed to be governed by a Board of Directors of nine members including the Secretaries of Agriculture, Labor, Public Works, and Education; the President of the Industrial Development Corporation and the General Manager of the Agricultural Bank. . . . The Board is encharged by law with establishing the policy, administrative organization, and functions of the Institute within the limits set by law. (Thome 1967: 26–27)

He reports, however, that in practice a director general of the IAD, or rather five different director generals within the five-year period he was reviewing (1962–67), had each assumed control while the board remained passive. It is also noted that within the IAD, continuity was lacking and paternalism was rampant.

In the original law, parcels of sufficient size for the maintenance and growth of a family were to be allocated to heads of households. Priority was to be given to those applicants who were already cultivating the land to be distributed, were displaced from their land as a result of agrarian reform projects, had significant experience in agriculture, were able to read and write, and were willing to participate in training and community development.

Parcels average approximately 50 *tareas* (15.9 *tareas* equal 1 hectare) and are assigned to the beneficiaries with provisional title only (Delgado 1983: 12). The state retains the right to withdraw the land in the case of inadequate performance on the part of the beneficiary, or in the case of abandonment by the beneficiary of his family or of the parcel of land. In most cases, if this were necessary, rights to the parcel would be extended to the wife or the son of the beneficiary. Parcels may not be sold or rented without the consent of the IAD, although family members may inherit the usufructuary rights. After sufficient time, and with completion of payment for the land, beneficiaries were to be given full title to the land.

Sources of Agrarian Reform Lands and Early Progress

The bulk of the land for distribution initially consisted of public land formerly owned by Trujillo and his family, as well as some donations by the recently formed State Sugar Corporation. Privately owned lands may be purchased by the IAD and distributed with the approval of the president of the Republic, although when the reform began it was not general policy. The colonization projects of earlier years were transferred to the IAD, as was the power to collect the "cuota parte"[1] lands in payment for irrigation services.

Given the sudden coup in September of 1983 and occupation by U.S. military forces in 1965, the reform made little progress in the first few years. However, although Bosch spent only six months as president, during that time he took actions to further the agrarian reform, including the application of the *cuota parte* law. David Stanfield notes that "of particular interest to Bosch was the productive riceland, and he managed to create several asentamientos, or settlements, composed of individual rice producing parcels on relatively productive land."[2]

After Joaquín Balaguer was elected president in 1966, there was a significant increase in the expropriation of land. Thome, in his 1967 report to AID comments that

> the President [Joaquín Balaguer] has, at various times and on his own initiative, ordered the purchase or expropriation of private properties for their subsequent redistribution, without bothering to consult the IAD or seek its advice. This action is apparently taken because the President considers that the land redistribution is proceeding too slowly, particularly in view of the fact that the rural population was one of his main supports in the last election. While these lands are then turned over to the IAD for distribution, these

transactions in effect constitute a "President's" land reform, separate and independent from that being carried out by the IAD. (Thome 1967: 31-32)

Balaguer's enthusiasm for agrarian reform continued throughout his 12-year administration. In 1972 further legislation passed that defined lands under the categories of *latifundios* and *baldios* (excessively large farms and lands not in production, respectively), which were then also subject to expropriation.

Table 3.2 documents the sources of the lands turned over to the IAD between 1962 and 1985.

A Multiplicity of Government Agencies

A major problem encountered in agrarian reform, mentioned by Thome, is the lack of coordination and cooperation between the various government agencies who participate, along with IAD, in the rural development effort (Thome 1967: 39-40). Among these other institutions specifically devoted to the agricultural sector are the Secretary of Agriculture (SEA), the major agricultural institution of the state; the Agricultural Bank (Banco Agrícola), the primary source of credit for the agricultural sector; the National Institute of Hydraulic Resources (INDRHI), encharged with constructing and maintaining irrigation systems; and the Price Stabilization Institute (INESPRE), responsible for the commercialization and stabilization of the prices of primary commodities. Two other government institutions involved in rural development are the Institute for Cooperative Development and Credit (IDECOOP), whose major efforts are to go to fomenting and establishing credit cooperatives and the Community Development Office (ODC), involved in technical assistance in a variety of areas. The majority of these institutions were established in 1962 and 1963 soon after the death of Trujillo, with the exception of INESPRE, which was established in 1969.

Carlos Aquino González, secretary of agriculture of the Dominican Republic from 1973 to 1975, agrees with Thome on this point in his 1978 book *Fundamentos para una Estrategia de Desarrollo Agrícola*, as does Francisco Rodríguez, ex-director general of the IAD, in a interview conducted in July of 1987.[3] Both men emphasize that many functions of the agencies overlap and also that coordination is made more difficult by lack of long-term planning. For example, the major responsibility of technical assistance and extension, within the agricultural sector, lies with the SEA; however, numerous agencies have extension-service functions including the Banco Agrícola, IAD, INDRHI, ODC, and IDECOOP. Additionally, although it is the major responsibility of the Banco Agrícola to provide credit to the agricultural sector, and of IDECOOP to establish credit cooperatives, the IAD and the SEA also have credit programs. Finally, all five of the major agricultural institutions are involved in the collection of data, such that for any agricultural datum that one might desire, it is usually possible to find five different figures.

Table 3.2

Area of Land Turned Over to IAD for Subsequent Distribution, According to Legal Form of Captation, 1962–85 (in hectares)

Years	State Lands	Donations of CEA	Land Purchases	Cuota Parte	Baldios & Latifundios	Public Utility	Private Donations	Totals
1962–71	6284	465	1566	0	0	0	742	9058
1972	1686	0	849	0	547	0	189	3271
1973	302	0	1786	57	1931	0	63	4139
1974	5994	0	277	315	7976	0	0	14562
1975	1239	0	270	94	1535	0	69	3208
1976	4315	38	208	126	5535	0	57	10278
1977	0	0	6	151	19	38	0	214
1978	195	283	164	6	528	189	82	1447
1979	403	0	264	31	0	434	0	1132
1980	333	0	50	31	0	182	321	918
1981	950	57	270	6	0	69	321	1673
1982	224	0	38	9	23	20	202	517
1983	510	0	337	38	0	90	46	1020
1984	183	0	113	126	0	0	177	598
1985	744	0	22	200	0	43	9	1019
Totals	23361	843	6222	1191	18095	1065	2278	53054

Sources: For 1962–81, Delgado, 1983, p. 149 taken from CALA, *Memoria 1976* (Santo Domingo, 1977), Cuadros 1–2 for 1962–71, and from IAD, División de Estudios Agronómicos y Oficina de Planificación, Sección de Estadística. For 1982–85, IAD, *Boletín Informativo Anual, 1985*.

Compounding these problems is the fact that the various institutions divide the country into sections of different shapes and sizes; for example, the Banco Agrícola has *surcusales*, the SEA has *regionales*, the IAD has *gerencias*, and the INDRHI has *distritos*—none of which coincide. This makes the coordination of activities all the more difficult and decreases substantially the usefulness of data collected. Whether these problems of coordination are causes of, or fruits of, what Rodríguez reports to be intense jealously between the institutions, can be debated. The need, however, for consolidation and reform within these institutions is hardly questionable.

The Banco Agrícola

The institution with, perhaps, the most well defined role in the agrarian reform sector is the Banco Agrícola. In recent years, though, an arm of the Central Bank, the Investment Fund for Economic Development (FIDE), which was created in 1966, has had increasing participation in extending loans to the agricultural sector.

Institutional credit increased considerably over the 1974–85 period (see Table 3.3). In 1975 it was estimated that only 54 percent of credit needs in the agricultural sector were satisfied through formal channels. By 1979 that figure had increased to 80 percent, and by 1981 a survey carried out by SEA estimates it at 89 percent.[4] Certainly the increase in loans from FIDE, of DR$5,600,000 to DR$89,400,000 in 1985 (shown in Table 3.3), accounts for satisfying a large part of the former deficit.

Table 3.3
Institutional Sources for Agricultural Credit

	Total Credit (000 DR$)	As Percentages of the Total:		
		BAGRICOLA	FIDE	Privadas
1974	117382.5	57.94%	4.77%	37.29%
1975	145020.9	53.81%	19.03%	27.16%
1976	151821.5	53.67%	4.87%	41.46%
1977	160201.2	52.12%	4.37%	43.51%
1978	188064.0	59.50%	9.04%	31.46%
1979	261922.3	62.72%	16.23%	21.05%
1980	263163.1	71.72%	16.95%	11.33%
1981	228220.0	65.44%	22.65%	11.91%
1982	284648.2	47.12%	18.97%	33.91%
1983	325709.9	49.11%	25.73%	25.16%
1984	386693.0	50.81%	15.23%	33.95%
1985	557915.7	43.11%	16.02%	40.87%

Source: Calculated from Banco Agrícola, *Boletín Estadístico, 1985*, p. 146.

Yet the Banco Agrícola remains the only institution approved by the IAD for loans to the agrarian reform sector, and in 1985 almost half of all loans formalized by the Banco Agrícola were destined to this sector.[5] Although agricultural loans from the Banco Agrícola are at subsidy rates (11 percent annually for loans above DR$2000, and 9 percent annually for those less than DR$2000 with inflation at 11.17 percent (Bravo-Barros 1983: 41), there are still many problems associated with obtaining credit from the Banco Agrícola.

Aquino González (1978: 74–75) emphasizes that credit from the Banco Agrícola has followed the crops where prices are high, shifting to others when prices fall. He also discusses the role of the local money-lender in providing fast, flexible, reliable credit. He comments that pro-ducers continue to seek local moneylenders even when rates are very high (10 percent or more per month according to farmers interviewed in 1987) because of the "torpeza" of institutional credit. This "torpeza" is exem-plified in credit for production only, insufficient funds that arrive late, difficult refinancing, and annoying paperwork. Fernando Ferrán is quoted saying:

> The process to obtain a loan from the Agricultural Bank is complex and con-sumes much time. The Bank requires many documents, the most significant being the title that proves ownership of the land. . . . Once the farmer has fulfilled all of these requirements, he is seen immersed in a bureaucratic process of paperwork.[6] (Aquino González 1978: 77)

Political Organizations

Stanfield emphasizes that in addition to the government agencies, various "political and semi-political organizations" were also instrumental in the organization and mobilization of the Dominican peasantry to pres-sure for further agrarian reform in the 1960s and early 1970s. The Dominican Federation of Christian Agrarian Leagues (FEDELAC) is one of these organizations that he mentions as being particularly important. Another is the Junta for Agrarian Action (JUNAGRA). The former receives significant international support and also has connections with the Dominican Catholic Church and the Social Christian Party. The latter is connected with the Reformist Party of Balaguer (Stanfield 1986: 7–8).

RICE COLLECTIVES AND THE AGRARIAN REFORM LAWS OF 1972

The 1972 Laws

In 1972 some major changes were introduced in the agrarian reform process. Most importantly, a decision was made to reallocate much of the productive rice lands to agrarian reform beneficiaries who were to farm the land collectively under the close supervision of the IAD. Until that time, the land had always been distributed as individual plots and the participation of the IAD in the production process had been minimal. After 1978 all of the IAD settlements were of the collective form. Table 3.4 illustrates the shift to the collective form of production.

Table 3.4
Projects, Beneficiaries, and Area Distributed, Individual and
Collective, 1961–86

	Number of Projects		Families Benefitted		Land Distributed (Hectares)	
	Indiv.	Collect.	Indiv.	Collect.	Indiv.	Collect.
1927–61	40		11451		140797	
1962	4		863		3849	
1963	11		719		3985	
1964	8		2214		11535	
1965	–		–		–	
1966	5		321		2497	
1967	19		1901		9804	
1968	17		1447		6904	
1969	24		2057		9767	
1970	23		1345		5144	
1971	16		3621		23810	
1972	39		6498		37546	
1973	49	47	5592	2770	30561	10085
1974	17	3	1683	117	8719	388
1975	10	8	1108	822	4964	4560
1976	11	3	1336	1826	6666	4434
1977	3	–	139	–	445	–
1978	11	7	1440	1194	5795	4633
1979		9		1962		8303
1980		14		1986		7874
1981		27		3244		14957
1982		16		1556		5149
1983		38		4238		10205
1984		37		2611		5981
1985	11	38	729	3599		9967
1986		16		2120		3825
Total	318	263	44464	28045	312788	90360

Source: IAD, *Boletín Informativo Anual, 1986.*

Law 290 of March 1972 required that the land of any rice farms larger than 500 *tareas* (approximately 85 acres), which received the benefits of state irrigation projects, be transferred to the IAD. To some extent this was an extension of the previous law specifying a *cuota parte* in payment for irrigation services; but in this case, the land was to be purchased with 25 percent of the value in cash and the remainder in government bonds. Additionally, Law 391 of September 22, 1972, established the system by which the lands were to be farmed collectively under the direct supervision of the IAD, regarding both credit provision and production management. Provisional rights were given to membership in the collective, rather than to a specific parcel of land. As of April 16, 1974, when Law 657 was passed, the collective form of management was to be extended to those rice lands that had been assigned to individuals.

The Role of Rice

Rice plays two very important roles in the Dominican political-
economic scene. In the first place, it is a major market-basket item, con-
suming up to 20 percent of average household expenditures for the
lower-income groups (CAPA 1987: 10–35). Secondly, rice is a very
important cash crop, surpassed in value only by sugar cane, and exceed-
ing the value of the production of the other major exports—tobacco, coffee, and cocoa—since 1981 (SEA 1987: 181). It is a major employer of
wage labor, is highly capitalized and highly productive, and encompasses
a wide range of producer sizes. For these reasons, the politics surrounding
rice are controversial.

Price Controls

Government intervention in rice politics began with price controls
after the assassination of Trujillo. During the 1961–66 period, policy
lacked coherence because of the multiple changes in government. Prices
to the consumer were lowered in 1961 by a reduction in taxes. Then in
1963 they were lowered at the farm level. While this policy discouraged
production in the short run, as Luis Crouch (1981: 149) comments, in
the long run it may have had the effect of permanently luring consumers
away from root crops.[7] But there were price increases in 1964 and 1965
and renewed increases in production.[8]

Under the regime of Balaguer, prices were frozen for several years
(1966–72). At the same time, there were numerous subsidies to rice producers in the form of research and development, duty-free fertilizer
imports, and a large increase in the supply of subsidized agricultural
credit, much of which went into rice production, along with irrigation
projects to increase the cultivable area.

The Price Stabilization Institute was created in 1969 for the purpose
of stabilizing commodity price swings by buying and selling rice in domestic as well as international markets. Its first rice imports took place in
1972. Since that time, INESPRE began to consolidate its hold over the
rice trade and continued its heavy participation in rice marketing (see
Table 3.5).

Among the *campesinos*, INESPRE has perhaps the worst reputation
of any government institution. It is seen as a means by which the government can exploit the farmer. Aquino González (1978: 41–42) stresses
that this low opinion of the price-control policies of INESPRE is not
restricted to farmers, but is prevalent among local economists and agricul-
turalists as well. A 1984 World Bank report severely criticizes the low-
price policies of INESPRE, quoting a 16 percent negative protection
below world price in the 1973–82 period (World Bank 1984: 39). They
stress that although rice production increased rapidly from 1973 to 1979

(see Table 3.5), the export potential has been stifled by low domestic prices. Furthermore, they conclude that

> rice prices could have averaged 10 percent higher during the last 8 years. This would have reduced the incomes of the poorest 30 percent of consumers only by an estimated 1.3 percent; most people could have shifted their purchase into alternative, cheaper food staples. . . . higher rice prices probably would have had an increased impact on rural wages and employment, and therefore income, by substantially more. By depressing incomes of rural producers these policies have removed an incentive for the rural population to stay on the land and inadvertently stimulated rural-urban migration. (World Bank 1984: 44)

Rodríguez-Núñez and Delgado both emphasize the deterioration of the internal terms of trade of the agricultural sector in the 1975–81 period, when as a result of the energy crisis agricultural-input prices increased by as much as 400 percent (Rodríguez-Núñez 1983: 9), while agricultural prices remained constant. Table 3.6 presents the INESPRE price to farmers for the 1973–86 period and the estimated cost of rice production for the 1979–86 period. As can be seen from the table, in 1984 farmers received the first significant price increase in many years, from DR$27.35 to DR$42.16 per 100 kilograms of rice paddy. Although the cost of production was increasing rapidly at the same time, the fall in terms of trade for the rice farmers was alleviated slightly.

Table 3.5
Production, Consumption, and Imports of Rice (thousands of metric tons)

Year	Domestic Production	Consumption	INESPRE Sales	INESPRE Domestic Purchases	Imports
1973	177.3	217.6	88.6	63.6	29.6
1974	197.0	244.1	197.4	149.0	72.4
1975	210.6	259.5	197.6	138.9	49.4
1976	210.8	247.1	203.1	143.6	31.6
1977	200.9	251.8	215.1	175.6	64.4
1978	227.8	222.3	191.2	188.0	10.4
1979	258.1	274.4	252.4	218.4	0.0
1980	254.1	291.3	260.8	230.5	40.5
1981	258.5	257.7	236.7	221.6	62.9
1982	254.4	281.7	223.8	214.1	0.0
1983a	299.7	283.6	264.0	254.0	0.0

aProjected for 1983

Source: World Bank Report No. 4353-DO, p. 38, from INESPRE, *Plan Operativa, 1983.*

Table 3.6
INESPRE Support Prices for Rice, Cost of Production, and Terms of Trade

Year	Price DR$/100kg Rice Paddy	Estimated Cost per Tarea	Terms of Trade
1973	15.00		
1974	22.08		
1975	22.08		
1976	22.08		
1977	22.08		
1978	22.08		
1979	22.08	48.74	1.00
1980	25.42	60.81	0.92
1981	27.35	72.82	0.83
1982	27.35	73.20	0.82
1983	27.35	88.67	0.68
1984	42.16	129.41	0.72
1985	64.48	175.81	0.81
1986	61.25	192.42	0.70

Sources: Juan José Espinal, *La Política de Precios Agrícolas: Su Incidencia en la Oferta de Alimentos*, Santo Domingo: Taller, 1987; SEA, *Plan Operativa, 1987.*

In 1986, due to serious problems of insolvency, INESPRE was forced out of rice marketing. A 1987 study of the role of the state in rice marketing, made by the Consejo Nacional de Agricultura (CAPA), describes the problem as follows:

> At the end of the previous constitutional period 1982–1986, the INESPRE was completely bankrupt. It had a debt in the millions with the bank, the commercial sector and fundamentally with the rice millers. The INESPRE could not technically pay this debt without the help of the central government.
>
> Faced with this situation and under pressure from the different groups of the rice sector, the executive power put out the Decree 212 on Sept 14, 1986 . . . passing in this form the absolute control of the rice market to the Agricultural Bank.[9] (CAPA 1987: 5-1)

The Banco Agrícola was to control the marketing of rice for an interim period, during which time it should prepare for the opening-up of rice marketing to a free market.

Production Control

The decision by the 1972 Balaguer regime to turn the productive rice lands over to the IAD to be set up as collective farms was in large part for the added control over the production of rice. With prices kept low, production incentives were diminished. By intervening on the production side of the rice question as well, the state could attempt to pursue a self-sufficiency program in rice. Stanfield presents the argument of the cost superiority of the peasant enterprise and the logic of Balaguer's decision:

> The individual peasant producer would be willing to produce food at lower prices than the capitalist producers, basically because of the peasant producers' allegedly lower opportunity costs. Balaguer and his advisors accepted the cost argument, but rejected the individual peasant enterprise as the most appropriate production unit. Rather they concluded that the individual peasant producer could not be depended upon to produce sufficient rice at low price levels. (Stanfield 1986: 19)

Further justification for the move into rice for agrarian reform could be found in the fact that many of the large rice producers had accumulated very large debts to the Banco Agrícola. The rice producers were also required to pay to INDRHI the cost of the water delivered. Large debts were left unpaid to both the Banco Agrícola and INDRHI. One benefit to the state of the collective form of enterprise was that debts to INDRHI and the Banco Agrícola could be deducted before profits were distributed to the agrarian reform beneficiaries.

Finally, it was considered necessary, given the high level of peasant unrest and frequent land invasions, to take significant steps toward increased equality in the agricultural sector. Since the rice lands included the most productive agricultural lands used for consumption crops in the country, distributing them to the peasants made for a significant gesture at the very least. In 1981 the average beneficiary of rice lands could earn three times as much income as the typical non-rice agrarian reform beneficiary, while the most fortunate rice beneficiary could earn up to ten times as much as the least fortunate non-rice beneficiary with the same 3 hectares of land.

The Importance of the Reform Sector in Rice

The IAD soon came to play a very major role in rice production in the Dominican Republic. In recent years, 35–40 percent of the country's rice output has been produced by the agrarian reform sector.[10] And within the agrarian reform sector, those *asentamientos* producing rice have received the bulk of government resources in terms of credit and technical assistance. In 1986 the rice sector under IAD management received 84.8 percent of all Banco Agrícola credit to IAD *asentamientos* even though the value of the production in the rice sector was only 56 percent of the total value of IAD production.[11]

Furthermore, the reports of Oscar Delgado (1983) and Pablo Rodríguez-Núñez (1985) reveal that the collective rice farms have contributed approximately 40 percent of IAD rice production in the 1975–83 period.[12] Both reports also emphasize that the bulk of the institutional resources in terms of credit and technical assistance, directed to the reform sector, have been focused on the collective *asentamientos*.

DEMANDS FOR THE ASSOCIATIVES: A TIME TO EVALUATE

The Collective-Individual Debate

Despite substantial institutional support for the collective farms, peasant response to the collective form of management for the IAD *asentamientos* has never been very positive. In fact, military forces were used at times to establish the collectives. By 1982, however, the opposition had become much more intense and the rice collectives were in the center of the controversy.

At present in the Dominican Republic the arguments in favor of and opposed to the collective form of farm management proceed along the same lines as those reviewed in Chapter 1. Essentially the *parceleros* object to the collective form because the equal division of profits suppresses individual initiative and also because of the administrative problems of internal organization. Institutions such as the IAD, the SEA, and the Banco Agrícola recognize the economies of scale in the provision of credit and technical assistance, as well as the control mechanism the collective provides over water resources, credit recuperation, and selective production.[13]

Stanfield (1986) reviews the local intellectual debate, citing, on the collective side, Carlos Aquino González, secretary of agriculture from 1973 to 1975; and, on the pro-individual side, Jorge Munguía, professor of economics at the Pedro Enríquez Ureña National University. Munguía argues that there are few, if any, economies of scale in agriculture but that in fact there are diseconomies of scale. One of the diseconomies mentioned is the separation of management from the land and the production process. The other is the "free-rider" problem of low worker incentive because compensation is not directly related to work done. At a more qualitative level, Munguía also argues that as individual entrepreneurs, peasants are in a much better position to develop their capacities than they are as laborers in a collective farm.

Aquino, on the other hand, points out economies of scale in purchasing and marketing, machinery use, and infrastructure. He speaks out for the role of the state in providing the discipline necessary to achieve these benefits rather than having them provided by a service cooperative. Finally, Aquino stresses the role that the state can play in encouraging new technology and thereby keeping production high on the collective and prices low for the consumers.

Beneficiaries Demand an Associative Compromise

Because of continuing fierce opposition by the beneficiaries to the collective system, steps were taken to improve the administrative apparatus of the collective rice farms. Stanfield (1986: 48–55) describes the progression of these efforts. A "Commission for the Evaluation of the

Rice Asentamientos of IAD" was created, and in 1975 it issued a report that stated that for the year 1974, productivity, access to credit, and use of improved rice varieties were all higher on the collective rice farms. Consequently they recommended not only that the collective model be maintained with some improvements, but that it be extended to those rice *asentamientos* assigned on an individual basis. Pressure from the beneficiaries continued, however, and many of the larger farms were divided into smaller units.

In 1979 a movement by the IAD to encourage greater worker participation began with the formation of Peasant Agrarian Reform Enterprises.[14] Stanfield reports that this attempt was met with considerable skepticism by *campesinos*. Workshops and seminars were organized to convince the beneficiaries of the advantages of the collective model; still they were not convinced.

In October of 1982 a letter was drafted by a committee from two rice-producing associations in the northwest, Padre Cavero and Gregorio Luperón from Rincón and Cotuí respectively, to President Jorge Blanco, the general director of the IAD, and to the secretary of agriculture, proposing an associative form of organization to replace the collective form (Stanfield 1986: 52–53). With the proposed associative form, each beneficiary would be responsible for his own parcel of land, while some activities, including the provision of credit, would be handled collectively. At that time many of the rice collectives were de facto reorganized into associatives. Finally, in March of 1985, Law 269 was passed legalizing the reorganization of the collectives and encouraging the formation of associatives by those assigned individual rights.

Efforts to Evaluate the Collective and Individual Forms

Before the legalization of the associatives in 1985, several studies focusing on the rice sector within the agrarian reform lands were done to try to come to some conclusion about the differences in productivity between the individual and collective rice settlements. These studies include Oscar Delgado 1983; Pablo Rodríguez-Núñez 1985; and Carlos Bravo-Barros 1983. No definitive results were obtained. Delgado concludes thus:

> It has not been possible to verify a significant incidence of the form of production, individual or collective, on the yields and the productivity, even when the effective personal income of the farm is more on the individuals than on the collectives. In the latter, economies of scale were found neither in the production . . . nor in the income. . . . Nevertheless, the collective receives more institutional support and subsidies than those received by the individuals. Moreover, its administration entails social costs more elevated than the control or the supervision of the individuals.[15] (Delgado 1983: 26)

The results of Rodríguez-Núñez do not agree with Delgado's claim that the individual settlements have higher net income. He finds, however, that during the seven-year period from 1975 to 1981 productivity averages, per beneficiary as well as per hectare, were higher on the collectives; whereas over the 1980 to 1981 period, these averages were higher on the individual farms. Based on these latter results, Stanfield emphasizes the relative deterioration in the collective model in Table 3.7.

Table 3.7
Indicators of Rice Production on Collective and Individual Settlements, 1975–76 and 1980–81

Indicator	Individual 1975–76	Individual 1980–81	% chg	Collective 1975–76	Collective 1980–81	% chg
Area harvested (000's ha)	27.8	26.7	–4%	9.6	16.5	+71%
Production (000's qq)	834.0	1184.0	+42%	541.0	716.0	+32%
Production per ha. (qq)	30.2	43.7	+45%	58.1	43.3	–25%
Production per benefic. (qq)	130.0	206.0	+58%	197.0	178.0	–10%

Note: 1 qq = 100 lbs
Source: Stanfield, 1986, p. 43.

The study of Carlos Bravo-Barros is based on a survey, sponsored by the FAO along with the IAD, taken in September and October of 1982, of 1392 beneficiary families from the two major rice-producing areas in the country: Yuna-Camú and Yaque del Norte. Bravo-Barros reports that the area surveyed covers 84 percent of the IAD rice area—99 percent of the collective rice area and 65 percent of the individually assigned area (Bravo-Barros 1983: 78–79). Relative to the total number of rice beneficiaries reported by Rodríguez-Núñez for 1981 (9903), the number of families surveyed represents only 14 percent of the total.

The study uncovers the interesting fact that only 34 percent of the families identified as collective beneficiaries were actually farming collectively (Bravo-Barros 1983: 109). Indeed, 66 percent belonged to collectives restructured into some variant of the associative model later instituted by law, which Bravo-Barros termed nominal collectives. Bravo-Barros also reports the desire to do so in all of those collectives that had not restructured (Bravo-Barros 1983: 112).

The results show a higher net profit per *parcelero* and per *tarea* on the nominal collective settlements than either the collective or the individual settlements. This is demonstrated in Table 3.8.

Table 3.8
Net Profit in Rice by Type of Settlement, per Beneficiary, and per Available Tarea (1981 DR$)

Type of Settlement	Total Net Profit	Net Profit/ Beneficiary[a]	Net Profit/ Available Tarea[b]
Individual	390,161	1,675	41.90
Collective	739,954	1,878	48.10
Nominal Collective	1,795,072	2,346	49.90

[a]Refers to net profit per family that was found in the sample: 233 families in individual settlements, 394 in collective settlements, and 765 families in nominal collectives.
[b]Available *tarea* refers to the *tareas* which can be cultivated or the area planted in the spring.

Source: Bravo–Barros, 1983, p. 110, Cuadro No. 47.

Factors that Cloud the Comparison

A number of factors cloud the comparison between the individual and collective rice settlements. As pointed out in the quote from Delgado, technical assistance and subsidies in the form of cheap credit have been concentrated on the collectives, many of which have reorganized into associatives. Rodríguez-Núñez also maintains that the soil quality is better on these farms. Additionally, the objectives of individual and collective settlements may not be the same. Individual beneficiaries would be most concerned with maximizing household income, while the IAD administrators of the collectives are under pressure from the state to maximize production. Thus, land productivity comparisons, as a measure of success of one form over another, are not entirely adequate.

Finally, as brought out by Bravo-Barros, without a survey it is impossible to determine precisely the form of organization. Since the collectives have reorganized spontaneously since their creation and, as we shall see in the next section, many of the individual settlements have also associated, comparison of the individual and collective settlements over several years on a national level, as in the attempts of Delgado and Rodríguez-Núñez, cannot be valid without careful documentation of all the changes in organizational structure.

To recapitulate, the chapter has thus far brought us up to date on the progression of agrarian reform, including a brief review of its complex institutional framework and the reasons for the recent controversy focused on the rice sector. Following next is a discussion of the workings of the individual, collective, and new associative settlements in more detail, with reference to specific rice projects in the northwest.

CASE STUDIES OF THE RICE PROJECTS

In 1983 the Land Tenure Center at the University of Wisconsin, Madison, in conjunction with the IAD and the Instituto Superior de

Agricultura (ISA), an agricultural research institute in Santiago, D.R., conducted research into the organizational structure of the agrarian reform projects. Since the rice sector has been the most controversial, case studies of particular rice projects in the northwest were undertaken to try to isolate the positive and negative aspects of the individual, collective, and associative forms of project management. Later, in 1985, further research was conducted by the Land Tenure Center in collaboration with the ISA and the Instituto Tecnológico de Santo Domingo under contract with the Consejo Nacional de Agricultura, R.D. The methodology used was based on interviews with members of the *asentamientos* as well as personnel from the relevant institutions.[16]

In June and July of 1987 this author revisited some of the projects studied by the aforementioned research teams for follow-up work on the success of the switch to the associative form of organization. This section is based on the results of that work and also draws on a thesis submitted to the ISA on two examples of the associative model, one which had previously been collectively farmed and another in which the land had been distributed as individual parcels.[17]

A total of six cases in the Mao-Valverde and San Francisco de Macorís regions are reviewed: three where individual *parceleros* have associated, and three cases of collectives now functioning as associatives. The former individual projects include Padre Fantino in Peasant Settlement No. 18 (AC–18), Rincón; Sergio A. Cabrera, AC–14, Camú; and El Esfuerzo, AC–25, Jaibón-Laguna Salada. The former collective projects include Vásquez Quintero in the Zona Arrocera Rincón, Finca Bermúdez in the Zona Arrocera Mao-Valverde (this farm later divided into two, A and B), and the association Santa Clara in the Zona Arrocera Rincón, composed of three former collective farms—Carlos Castillo I and II and Reynaldo Bisonó. Some basic data relevant to these cases is summarized in Table A.4 in the Appendix.

In what follows, a brief characterization of the individual and collective management forms is provided before exploring in more detail the new organizational structure that has arisen from the individual and collective projects.

The Individual and Collective Projects

The individual settlements are characterized by very low participation from the IAD. Stanfield and others report the following:

> In many of the traditional individual asentamientos, there is no IAD resident administrator or supervisor. The parceleros are mostly on their own, unless someone complains to IAD about some possible violation of the law. Some colonies have been left alone so long that much of the land has changed hands without official recognition or approval. (Stanfield et al. 1986: 7)

Due to low agency participation, access to technical assistance is very limited for the individual beneficiaries and their adoption of new technology is low.

A further consequence of the lack of administrative assistance is that the individual *parceleros* have considerable difficulty negotiating with the Banco Agrícola for loans, with the INDRHI for timely provision of water services, and arranging tractor services for land preparation and for harvest. Additionally, each one must negotiate his own sale of rice to INESPRE or to a miller regulated by INESPRE, as well as his own purchases of inputs from private companies. The difficulty involves not only the lack of bargaining power as one small farmer but also the high cost of time involved in making trips to the bank and the other institutions.

Farming as individuals, many of the beneficiaries are left without access to credit from the Agricultural Bank. Stanfield and others reveal that although beneficiaries in Padre Fantino received credit initially, soon many of them were considered to be too great a credit risk:

> The individual parceleros obtained credit from the Agricultural Bank, but their production levels were low and much of the production was used for feeding the family members of the beneficiaries. Many parceleros could not repay their debts, and the Bank ended credit to many, continuing to lend individually to those parceleros who paid back their loans. (Stanfield et al. 1986: 8)

For the farmers, the alternative to credit from the Agricultural Bank is credit from the rice millers at rates of 10 percent or more per month.

The collective rice farms, on the other hand, received considerable attention from the IAD, as well as the bulk of the credit from the Banco Agrícola that was appropriated to the reform sector. They were governed by an administrative council, including an elected representative of the *parceleros*, a representative of the executive branch, and an administrator from the IAD. Committees were in charge of production, credit, purchasing, marketing, discipline, and social affairs. The IAD administrator had veto power over the others, as well as the power to dismiss any beneficiary who was not performing his duties properly. Initially, collectives varied in size from 60 to 80 members, and profits were divided among the beneficiaries according to days worked.

The major complaints voiced by the beneficiaries on the collective projects focused on three major problems: the lack of relationship between work done by members and payment received, excessive control by the IAD administrator, and the inability of the collective farm to absorb family labor.

Although workers were paid according to days worked and a "listero" was in charge of keeping track of who works when, this did not provide an effective control. Due to the difficulty of accusing friends of feigning illness or docking a neighbor for running an errand in town, in general everyone was reported as having worked every day and profits were divided equally. Additionally, since work was counted in days rather than hours, everyone was to start working at the same time. This caused significant delay at the beginning of each workday.

The amount of effort each beneficiary puts into his time at work is even more difficult to police. The studies of Carlos Castillo and Vásquez Quintero report the great enthusiasm with which the collectives began to work. One member of Vásquez Quintero is quoted recalling, "When they gave us the land it was like giving something to eat to a man dying of hunger. We entered with a fever to work!"[18] (Gutiérrez 1983b: 6). But the difficulty of maintaining equal effort from all parties has led to lower effort by all in the longer run. Attempts to improve the incentive problem led to the division of many of the collectives into smaller farms, as in the cases of Carlos Castillo I and II and in Bermúdez A and B, where the original farms were divided in half after three and ten years of working, respectively.

The IAD administrator played a key role in the success, or lack thereof, of any collective reform project. Carter and Kanel, in their study of the case of Finca Bermúdez, discuss differences between various supervisors and the effect that they had on the functioning of the collective farm. At the time of the study in 1983, Finca Bermúdez was one of the more successful collective projects. The administrator was considerably more passive than those in the past and performed the critical role as liaison to government agencies without imposing his will on the decision-making process. Local leadership was active and strong and provided the key to the successful operation of the project. This had not always been the case, though. In general, the IAD administrator has played a very strong policy-making role, such as deciding investments plans with the Banco Agrícola.

Unfortunately, there is a natural divergence in the objectives of the IAD administrator from those of the beneficiaries. The former is concerned with moving up in the bureaucracy in which he works and the latter with maximizing net income to their households. This, added to the fact that turnover of administrators is very high, has made for a lack of continuity in policy.

Additionally, the government goals for self-sufficiency in rice were imposed on the beneficiaries by the administrators. This problem came up in the decision of what kind of rice to plant: the new high-yielding variety that must be planted twice a year or the old standard that gives a good *retoño* or second crop, without having to be replanted. The administrators preferred the high-yielding variety to satisfy their superiors. The beneficiaries, however, recognized the lower cost and less work necessary for the other and, especially when faced with low prices in rice, often found it to be the better choice.

Finally, the inability of the collectives to absorb family labor was one of the more serious complaints of the *parceleros*. The difficulty of determining how to remunerate family members fairly, without underpaying or overpaying and causing jealousy among members, effectively excluded family members from the work force. On individual parcels, low opportunity cost family labor is an important source of farm labor and is utilized until the marginal product is equal to zero.

The Associatives as a Compromise

For the above-mentioned reasons, in 1982 and 1983 a number of collective rice settlements in the northwest distributed the land to the members as individual parcels and reorganized according to the proposed associative form.

The original letter to Jorge Blanco from the soon-to-be associatives recommended that land preparation, credit from the Banco Agrícola, irrigation, purchase of fertilizers, and aerial application of insecticides be carried out associatively, but that "work, sale and payment be individual" (Stanfield et al. 1986: 53). They also suggested that the administrative council be made up of a representative from the IAD, another from the Banco Agrícola, and a third from the SEA, along with three to five *parceleros.* With such a spontaneous reorganization, however, the precise structure of the projects varied from case to case, depending upon the local leadership. When Law 269 passed in 1985 legalizing the associative form, it specified that profits be divided according to the production of each beneficiary, that the administrative council be composed of two elected beneficiaries and a representative from IAD who should promote self-management of the project by the beneficiaries. Rather than detailing the precise structure of the associative, the law stated that the IAD should be flexible in legalizing various forms of organization.

While the collective farms have expressed a strong desire to manage the land as individual units, retaining some collective activities, there are many examples of individual *asentamientos* associating to capture advantages of group effort. For associations like Padre Fantino, Sergio A. Cabrera, and El Esfuerzo, the motives to associate were political as well as economic. Foremost among these were the cost savings obtained on collective purchase of inputs and the increased bargaining power vis-à-vis government and private agencies.

The members found that not only could they obtain better prices on inputs, such as seed and fertilizer, but due to the increased status of the association, the service and quality of the products were better as well. Additionally, only one person had to sacrifice labor hours to go to town to do the negotiating. The high transaction cost of obtaining credit from the Banco Agrícola—including documentation and legal fees, administrative costs, transportation, time and opportunity cost—was also reduced by obtaining one collective loan. Finally, they could diminish the inconvenience of arranging for tractor services in the community with the purchase of capital equipment by the association.

Administrative Structure

Although the basic administrative structure throughout associative projects is similar—that is, a board of directors including president, vice-president, secretary, treasurer, and committees for purchases, marketing, credit, and so on—in practice there is wide variation in which officer actually performs the various administrative duties.

For example, in the association Sergio A. Cabrera, established in 1980 with 63 members who had been assigned individual parcels in 1964, the president plays a central role. This post involves planning and organization, coordinating the efforts of the committees and motivating the members, and managing commercial business with public and private agencies, as well as acting as the representative of the association whenever called upon. Committees are responsible for marketing, including coordinating purchases and rice sales and arranging transport; for credit, involving coordinating with each farmer and the Banco Agrícola to take into account the financial requirements of all; and also for technical supervision, focusing on the sequencing of the tractor services. Officers are elected for a two-year term. Members are to pay for inputs used, marketing charges (one peso per sack of rice),[19] interest as well as a service charge on the credit they obtained, and fees per *tarea* for the use of the machinery and irrigation services. The board of directors receives a salary, and the association hires an accountant and office secretary.

In Padre Fantino, however, also established in 1980 with 59 members who had been assigned individual parcels in 1963, there is no salary for the board of directors even though administrative structure is very similar to that of Sergio A. Cabrera. Each member pays DR$100[20] per harvest to cover administrative costs, including marketing costs and salary for an accountant. Purchasing in both of these two projects is undertaken by the president.

A final ex-individual project, El Esfuerzo, founded in 1978 with 59 members, and studied by Genao and Torres (1987), is reported to be dominated by the board of directors. Although a purchasing committee exists, the secretary does this job while the president and treasurer handle credit and marketing. The only committee that functions apart from the board is that in charge of machinery. No mention is made of compensation.

The variation in administrative structure among the former collective projects is even more surprising given that they were originally all organized under the direction of the IAD.

The farm Vásquez Quintero, established with 63 members in 1973 after an application of the *cuota parte* law, began functioning as an associative at the beginning of 1983, maintaining essentially the same structure as it had as a collective. In other words, it has an administrative council where effectively the president and an IAD administrator manage the production plan and handle credit with the help of the credit committee. Marketing and purchasing committees carry out their respective functions. Other committees include production, discipline, and social affairs, but they are largely inoperable. Members pay DR$15 per harvest to the marketing committee to cover costs, DR$35 per harvest for irrigation services, and DR$25 per harvest for salaries of the president and the accountant, and to cover costs of the credit committee (Gutiérrez 1983b: 10). Costs are divided equally among members, since all have the same size parcel.

The association Santa Clara was formed in 1983 from collective farms Carlos Castillo I and II with 20 beneficiaries each, and Reynaldo Bisonó with 48 beneficiaries, all established in 1973. While each group continues to have their individual administrative structure, the association has a board of directors consisting of a president, vice-president, secretary of discipline, secretary of acts, secretary of organization, and committees for purchasing and marketing as well as vigilance. Members contribute to cover administrative costs according to the amount of land they hold. Because the association (since 1986) owns and runs a rice mill with financing from the FAO, it pays salaries to employees of the mill, including an accountant and an administrator. The three groups may carry out activities of their own, but the association as a whole handles credit and purchasing (for this the association hires another accountant). Although the marketing committee makes recommendations as to where members should sell their rice, each is free to sell on his own, or within his group.

The collective Finca Bermúdez, initially composed of 88 members when established in 1974, divided into farms A and B with 44 members each at the end of 1982 and not too long thereafter began functioning as two associative farms. Genao and Torres (1987) report that Bermúdez A is essentially run by the president (or beneficiary representative who is a member of the administrative council along with an IAD administrator) and the heads of the committees of purchasing, marketing, and credit. Members were contributing DR$75 per harvest to cover salaries of these four men, who then decided, without opposition in 1986, to increase that amount to DR$100 (Genao and Torres 1987: 52). In Bermúdez B the president and treasurer share the bulk of the work and both receive salaries. Committees exist for production, marketing, purchasing, and discipline. Officers and committee personnel may be rotated after six months if they are not working out well; they may remain in their post up to five years otherwise.

The variation in administrative structure reflects differences in group dynamics and personalities involved and the particular process of adaptation that each group has undergone to find the most effective structure. It is interesting to note that the former collectives are really no more different from the former individual projects than one former collective is from another.

Agency Participation

When it comes to agency participation, all the associations agree that there is much to complain about. The loudest complaints regard the fact that the beneficiaries must pay the INDRHI for maintaining irrigation canals and the IAD for maintenance of roads and bridges but that in fact these services are not provided. Extension agents from the IAD substantiate these claims. In regard to technical assistance, the administrator of the rice mill of the association Santa Clara, who goes by the name of Guarín, commented, "All the agencies have technical assistance personnel and not one is worth anything."[21] Luis Castro, a leader for 23 years with the group from Sergio A. Cabrera, was a little more gracious to the *agrónomo* from the IAD who was present in both conversations, admitting that occasionally a good *técnico* appeared—perhaps from IAD, perhaps from SEA. Others interviewed agreed that they did receive technical assistance at times from one or the other of these two institutions. Although they may not have been fully satisfied with the services provided, they seemed in no hurry to further alienate the agency personnel.

The aforementioned *agrónomo*, José Sicard, had worked for the IAD in the San Francisco de Macorís zone with rice projects—collective and individual—for 14 years and was actually rather well respected as *agronomos* go. He made some effort to defend himself and his peers, protesting that the IAD as an institution did not provide the necessary resources with which to work, "No hay gasolina!"[22] For an *agrónomo* on a small salary, there is very little incentive for him to pay out of his own pocket for the transportation that the IAD is obliged to provide, in order to go out to the field when there is nothing in it for him other than the appreciation (if he's lucky) from the beneficiaries. Guarín agreed that it really was not the fault of the *agrónomos* themselves, but rather the politics of the institutions they worked in. He suggested, additionally, that the hierarchy in the government would prefer that the land reform not be successful. Later, when questioned about the lack of incentives to complete his job, Sicard admitted that he did have a small private consulting business on the side.

There is one government agency, however, that is viewed as essential by even the most skeptical reform beneficiary, and that agency is the Banco Agrícola. No one wants to go without the credit provided by the government, although there are complaints that it sometimes arrives late.

Supervision of that credit by an administrator outside the local community is regarded as a valuable service. Gumesindo Gómez, a leader for many years with Padre Fantino, suggested that they get rid of all the other government agencies except the Banco Agrícola.

Credit Problems

This is certainly not to say that the service of providing credit to the members of the associations is carried out without problem. In fact it is a difficult and complex problem, and the associations are constantly looking for ways to improve the process.

Regarding the associative form of production, Article 4 of Law 269 in 1985, states that the group's administrative council (two beneficiary representatives along with an IAD administrator) will be responsible to solicit from the Agricultural Bank or any other credit institution considered appropriate the funds required for production or investment activities, that this credit will be backed by the guarantee of the state, and that the administrative council is further responsible for the supervision of these funds. Gutiérrez explains how the group credit is handled and who is responsible:

> Once the agents from the bank approved the global amount per *tarea*, they gave a contract for the total amount of the loan that they were requesting. They also prepared individual investment plans for each beneficiary. The Agricultural Bank delivered only one check to the association in representation of the individual members but each member contracted with the bank an individual debt according to his own investment plan.[23] (Gutiérrez 1983a: 12)

Even though the individuals are responsible to the bank, the association, rather than the bank, keeps an account for each member, as he makes withdrawals through the production period. The Agricultural Bank keeps only one account for the association.[24]

Stanfield and others (1983: 35) explain that although each beneficiary is responsible for his own debt, if some beneficiary experiences a loss and cannot pay, the association will pay the bank. Thus, the associative credit programs provide significant insurance benefits. The associations Vásquez Quintero and Sergio A. Cabrera have, as reported by Gutiérrez (1983a and 1983b), agreed that for a beneficiary who experiences a loss three times, the association would intervene in the management of the parcel until the loan was paid off and request to the IAD that this beneficiary be replaced by another.

Stanfield and others suggest, however, that although it is one thing to define the regulation on paper, it is another to actually implement. They point out that such a loss could be due to climatic factors and that it could be difficult to determine precisely whether this was in fact the case. Conflict within the group could result. They also direct their attention to another problem, that of long-term loans for capital equipment or other outstanding debt. They explain that although some beneficiaries may be able to pay off their part of the debt much earlier than others, the bank will continue to deduct from the total profit of the association until the debt is paid off. In the meantime, those who have more net benefits will carry the burden for those who have less (Stanfield et al. 1983: 35–36). Some beneficiaries in Padre Fantino have responded to these difficulties by not participating in the associative credit plan though they remain members of the association.

Another complication is that of the timing of the loan process. Gutiérrez discusses the fact that the Agricultural Bank does not release credit for the next production period until everyone has sold his last harvest (Gutiérrez 1983b: 12–13). This causes problems not only because many may experience liquidity problems during harvest, but also because not everyone plants at the same time. When the credit from the Agricultural Bank is not yet available, the alternative source of credit is from the rice millers or private usurers at rates of 3 percent weekly or 10 percent monthly.[25]

Guarín, the administrator of the rice mill owned by the association Santa Clara, was particularly aggravated by the credit situation, complaining that it required "dos meses de papeleo"[26] to get credit from the Agricultural Bank and even then it was insufficient, covering only 75 percent of what was needed. He remarked that although it was permitted by law, IAD had never yet authorized a private bank to lend, but that with the government guarantee, private banks should be interested in providing the credit that the Banco Agrícola is unable to. Stanfield and others report that indeed the private sector has expressed interest in financing the production of associations. They discuss the case of a fertilizer and pesticide company interested in financing the needs of the federation Padre Cavero, in the Rincón area, with 18 rice associatives in its membership:

> The company was willing to finance the costs of land preparation, planting, weeding and harvest, as well as the needed fertilizers and pesticides, with the only guarantee being the value of the rice produced and the good name of the Federation. Some sort of production contract may be worked out with the company to replace the Agricultural Bank and IAD, should the associations be able to become more independent of these two state agencies and itself enter into such contracts. (Stanfield et al. 1986: 17)

It will be interesting to see if the private sector is eventually allowed to enter the agrarian reform picture.

Capital Investment

Capital investment is another area where problems are encountered. The associatives have responded in a variety of ways to overcome these problems. Rosa Minebra Chávez relates an example of such a case in Bermúdez B. Formerly the association owned two tractors, but the ten people who took care of the tractors—drivers, mechanics, and so on—

were benefitting while the association was losing money on the tractors. Now those ten people own the tractors while the other members rent their services. The associations Padre Fantino and Sergio A. Cabrera, however, own quite a bit of capital equipment with fewer reported problems.[27] Members pay per *tarea* for tractor services; and of the money so collected, the association pays 40 percent to the bank to service the loan and 60 percent on operating costs.

Most of the associations interviewed report a combination of capital owned by the entire association, capital owned by small groups of two to four beneficiaries, and capital owned by individuals. The entire association, the small groups, and the individuals then receive payment from members who use the equipment. Guarín, of Santa Clara, reported that relative to the collective form of organization, the members were still quite willing to make investment together but that there was much more incentive now, as an associative, for individuals to make private investments as well.

The Role of Leadership

Finally, it is important to stress the critical role that local leaders have played in the process of reorganization. From this vantage point, it is easy to see the development of local leadership over almost 25 years of experience with agrarian reform projects. Men like Luis Castro of Sergio A. Cabrera and Gumesindo Gómez of Padre Fantino were among the wage laborers that participated in the land invasions at the death of Trujillo. They helped to form credit cooperatives and watched them fail, and they participated in courses offered by FEDELAC that took them as far from Ranchito and Rincón as Miami and Venezuela. Only such a strong core of local leaders who recognized the potential benefits could convince the other members to work together for their mutual betterment.

Among the collectives, the burden of responsibilities as officers and members of committees, though it was supposed to rotate, usually fell on the shoulders of a few. These local leaders received substantial education over the years. Although they may have needed the services of the IAD administrator in the earlier years, their more intense interest in the production process, and their desire for the progress of their community, eventually made them the more able administrators.

CONCLUSION

The relative benefits of communal and individual land tenure have been considered in the Dominican Republic since shortly after the arrival of Columbus. Currently, agrarian reform beneficiaries in the rice sector, and the institutions with which they work, are trying to find a compromise capable of reaping the benefits of association while still preserving the scope for individual initiative.

At the death of Trujillo, there was a complete lack of institutions to service the rural sector. Within a few years, however, a multiplicity of rural institutions arose, including the Instituto Agrario Dominicano, which administered the agrarian reform program. The land reform program was initiated while these institutions were still in their infancy. During the 25 years of agrarian reform, emphasis has shifted from individual parcels to collective farms, and now the pendulum is swinging back the other way.

In this chapter an effort has been made to lay the framework for the analytical study that follows, exploring the implications of the various organizational structures of the land reform projects in the rice sector of the Dominican Republic. Factors to be kept in mind are (1) the multiplicity of government agencies with whom the reform beneficiaries must negotiate and the consequent central role of the IAD administrator or perhaps preferably strong local leadership; (2) the potential benefits to associative action—including credit availability, increased bargaining power in purchasing and marketing, and improved access to capital equipment—when the administrative structure is properly motivated; (3) the intense desire on the part of the beneficiaries for control over their own plot of land.

NOTES

1. The "cuota parte" law specifies that those landowners who had benefitted from state irrigation projects were to give up a certain percentage of their land (usually 25 to 30 percent) to the state.

2. Stanfield 1986: 5–6. Stanfield gives an excellent review of agrarian reform in the Dominican Republic in Thiesenhusen 1989.

3. As well as serving as the director general of the IAD, Francisco Rodríguez has also served in IDECOOP, ODC, INDRHI, and ONAPLAN (Oficina Nacional de Planificación). This latter is responsible for coordination and planning between institutions but has little political power.

4. *Estudio de Base del Sector Agropecuario y Forestal*, Secretariado Técnico de la Presidencia, August, 1982, p. 178; Consejo Nacional de Agricultura, "El Financiamiento Agropecuario: El Déficit de la Oferta y Alternativas Viables," DP-UEA No. 001–84, November, 1984, p. 8.

5. Banco Agrícola, *Boletín Estadística*, 1985.

6. "El proceso para obtener un prestamo del Banco Agrícola es complejo y consume mucho tiempo. El Banco exige muchos documentos, siendo el más significativo el certificado de título que prueba la propiedad de la tierra. . . . Una vez que el campesino ha llenado estos requisitos, se ve inmerso en un proceso burocratico y de papeleo."

7. In fact, per capita consumption of rice has increased from 0.51 qq in 1962 to 1.25 qq in 1986 (see Table 6.1).

8. See Crouch 1981: 145–65 for a review of rice politics in the 1961–77 period.

9. "Al terminar el anterior período constitucional 1982–1986, el INESPRE quedó en la completa bancarrota. Tenía una deuda millonaria con la banca, el comercio y fundamentalmente los molineros. El INESPRE técnicamente no tenía posibilidades de pagar dicha deuda sin la ayuda del Gobierno Central.

"Ante esta situación y bajo la presión de los diferentes grupos del sector arrocero, el Poder Ejecutivo emitió el Decreto 212 en fecha 14 septiembre . . . pasando de esta forma el control absoluto del mercado del arroz al Banco Agrícola."

10. IAD annual bulletins.

11. 1986 IAD annual bulletin. See Table A.1 in the Appendix.

12. Delgado (1983: 170) and Rodríguez-Núñez (1985: 44) break rice production down into individual and collective production, but their figures differ substantially. Delgado's average collective contribution—approximately 35 percent—is lower than that of Rodríguez-Núñez—approximately 45 percent.

13. In the case studies of the following section, the objections of the *parceleros* to the collective farms will be taken up in more detail, as will the advantages they perceive to cooperative action.

14. Empresas Campesinas de la Reforma Agraria or ECRAs.

15. "No se ha podido verificar una incidencia significativa de la forma de producción, individual o colectiva, sobre los rendimientos y la productividad, aún cuando el ingreso personal en efectivo de la finca es major en los individuales que en los colectivos. En estos no fueron advertidas economías de escala, ni en la producción . . . ni en el ingreso. . . . Sin embargo, el colectivo recibe más apoyo institucional y subsidios que los percibidos por los individuales. Además, su administración comporta costos sociales más elevados que el control o la vigilancia de los individuales."

16. These studies include Stanfield and others 1983; Stanfield and others 1986; Stringer 1986; Carter and Kanel 1985; Gutiérrez 1983a and 1983b.

17. Genao and Torres 1987, thesis submitted to complete the degree of Ingeniero Agrónomo.

18. "Cuando nos dieron la tierra era como darle de comer a un muerto de hambre. Entramos con fiebre de trabajar!"

19. Reported in interviews with author, July 1987, Ranchito, D.R.

20. Reported in interviews with author, July 1987, Rincón, D.R.

21. "Todos las agencias tienen técnicos y ninguno sirve." These agencies include IAD, Banco Agrícola, INDRHI, SEA, and ODC, as described earlier.

22. "There's no gas."

23. "Una vez que los técnicos del Banco daban su aprobación al monto global por tarea, le pasaban a la Asociación un contrato por el

total del préstamo que se estaba pidiendo. Se preparaban también formularios individuales para el plan de inversión de cada parcelero. El BAGRICOLA entregaba un solo cheque a la Asociación en representacion de los socios individuales pero cada socio contraía con el Banco una deuda individual según su propio plan de inversión."

24. A further feature of many associative projects are life insurance and forced savings programs. For example, in Vásquez Quintero, every member would contribute DR$5 to the family of another member who had died (Gutiérrez 1983b: 10). In Padre Fantino (which also has a life insurance plan), 3 percent of every member's net benefits remains in the Agricultural Bank in savings, while 7 percent remains in the association as capital.

25. These figures are according to Luis Castro of Sergio A. Cabrera, as of July 1987.

26. "two months of shuffling papers"

27. Padre Fantino reportedly has two tractors, a truck, a harvester, and eight small tillers in addition to the warehouse and meeting place of the association.

4

Incentives, Organization, and Agricultural Contracts: The Issues

The essential elements involved in the organization of land reform projects have been developed in the earlier chapters—first in the context of agrarian reform in general in Latin America and then more specifically with regard to the rice sector in the Dominican Republic.

These elements include (1) the crucial role of credit for the small farmer to provide liquidity and mitigate risk, (2) the potential scale benefits to collectivization, (3) the inevitable free-rider problem with collectivization, (4) the key position of the agrarian reform agency administrator or local leader, and (5) the potential conflict of interest or divergence in incentives between the beneficiaries, administrator or local leader, and the government agency in charge. The desirability of finding a structure that captures the scale benefits of group effort while maintaining individual initiative has been demonstrated for the rice projects in the Dominican Republic as well as in Latin America in general.

Although a very large literature has been developed that applies the modern techniques in microeconomic theory to the problem of sharecropping in the eastern hemisphere and to the collective farms and enterprises in the Soviet Union and China, surprisingly little microtheoretic literature exists on the issues of land reform in Latin America. The present chapter will briefly review the germane literature before developing in the following chapter a simple model that captures those elements central to the problems of organizational structure of land reform projects in Latin America.

INCENTIVES AND ORGANIZATION THEORY

The Principal-Agent Problem

The basic literature exploring the problems of incentives and risk sharing between two parties focuses on the principal and agent relationship (Harris and Raviv 1979; Holmstrom 1979; Shavell 1979). A theory of contracts has developed to explain situations in which the information, incentives, and risk tolerance of the two individuals may differ.

In general the model specifies that output is a function of effort by the agent and some random variable. This output, which is publicly observable, is to be divided between the principal and the agent. Since the agent has disutility for effort, while the principal is indifferent to effort supplied by the agent (except for its contribution to output), incentive problems arise.

Because the agent chooses an effort level that is not observable by the principal and hence not enforceable, to maximize his utility over income and effort the principal must design a contract based on output such that the agent puts forth effort. When, however, the agent is more averse to risk than is the principal, basing the agent's income entirely on an uncertain output would lead to inefficient risk sharing. Hence the optimal contract must strike a balance between risk sharing and incentive considerations.

The "agency" relationship has been developed in terms of employer-employee, client-lawyer, owner-manager, and landlord-tenant situations, to name only a few, and has been studied under a variety of assumptions about information asymmetries, differences in risk aversion, and effort-monitoring possibilities.

Team Theory

Another important body of literature dealing with the structure of information and decision-making within an organization is the theory of teams as formulated by Jacob Marschak and Roy Radner (1972).

The basic team model abstracts from the aspect of incentives, assuming that the various members are guided by a common goal, to concentrate on the aspect of the distribution of information within the firm. The payoff function of the firm depends on the actions taken by the team members, whose decisions are based on information gathered through observations of the environment. These decisions are assumed to be random and vary across members. The objective is to determine optimal decision structures by the agents to maximize the payoff to the firm.[1]

Theodore Groves (1973) extended the model to include the problem of incentives. Under this formulation the head of the organization devises an incentive structure or set of compensation rules to induce the other members of the organization to behave as a team (that is, to make optimal decisions and truthfully reveal information). In this incentive structure each member's compensation will depend upon the total payoff to the firm and perhaps the payoff to his subunit. Both the Groves and the Marschak-Radner formulations emphasize the distribution and flows of information within the firm.

Hierarchies and Supervision

Yet another major vein of organization theory is that of hierarchies as formulated initially by Oliver Williamson (1967).

Williamson focuses his model on the role of supervision and shows how "control loss" across successive hierarchical levels limits the size of an organization. In this problem the only choice variable is the number of hierarchical levels, whereas the degree of employee compliance is assumed to be a parameter,[2] as is the number of employees a supervisor can manage effectively. These are taken to be parameters based on U.S. Department of Labor studies. No discussion is presented as to the obvious trade-off that might exist between loss of control and number of employees per supervisor, and no account is taken of incentives. Wages are fixed, and the labor input provided is determined by the number of employees each supervisor can handle.

Williamson's conclusions were challenged by Calvo and Wellisz (1978), as well as by Mirrlees (1976). In Calvo and Wellisz, workers choose their effort levels given some penalty associated with being checked by a supervisor while not performing adequately, and some probability of being checked. In this case the probability of being checked does depend on the number of workers per level. The problem of the firm owner is to choose the payment rule and the number of workers per hierarchical level to maximize firm profit.

Likewise in Mirrlees, supervisory efforts are choice variables of the organization head and the supervisors, as are payment rules. Maximization is carried out at successive supervisory levels subject to the maximization at earlier stages. Workers at the lowest stage choose their effort levels.

Common to these three formulations, as well as to a discussion by Stiglitz (1975), is the condition that only the workers at the lowest level contribute productive effort, whereas the function of successive hierarchical levels is purely supervisory.

THE ORGANIZATION OF AGRICULTURE: APPLICATIONS IN THE EASTERN HEMISPHERE

The Collective Farm in the Soviet Union and China

The Soviet collective farm is characterized by Domar (1966) as a producer cooperative following the original work of Ward (1958) based on the Yugoslav experience. The Domar-Ward model is one of perfect certainty where the supply of labor per worker (or worker household) is fixed and the number of workers is chosen to maximize average worker income. Output is collectively produced and profits are divided equally. Oi and Clayton (1968) expand the model to analyze the influence of private plots and production quotas. In all three the problem of worker incentive is avoided with the assumption of fixed labor per household.

Amartya Sen (1966) makes the work done per person variable to treat the problem of incentives under a contract where a certain proportion of income is distributed according to needs and the remainder according to labor applied. This still takes place in a world of certainty, where labor effort is publicly observable, and the problem is considered under varying degrees of "social consciousness" by use of a parameter that weights the utility that members derive from the satisfaction of other members.

More recently Louis Putterman (1980) and Putterman and DiGiorgio (1985) combine the two approaches of Sen and Oi-Clayton to study the significant question of whether self-interested peasants would ever voluntarily decide to unite their land and labor for collective production in the villages of Tanzania and China.

Under conditions of certainty and full information, a democratic vote determines the proportion of land to be devoted to collective production as well as the proportion of income to be distributed according to needs. Each member allocates his time between production on the private plot, collective production, and leisure. They find that collective production may indeed voluntarily be chosen by self-interested parties when sufficient economies of scale exist.

Finally, along another line, Weitzman (1976) analyzes incentive problems in the Soviet enterprise in relation to the system of targeted production, quotas, and bonuses. Given that such targets are necessary for proper coordination in a planned economy, bonus coefficients are chosen to provide incentives for managers to select optimal targets when output is uncertain.

Tenancy Contracts in India and Southeast Asia

Studies of the organization of agricultural production in India and Southeast Asia have focused on the form of tenancy arrangement. Given the classical conclusions that sharecropping results in a suboptimal application of labor, the widespread existence of share tenancy contracts has inspired a wealth of research as to why it might exist rationally (Cheung 1969) or how (by sharing costs as well as output) it might be improved upon to work efficiently (Adams and Rask 1968).

Steven Cheung's *The Theory of Share Tenancy* is an in-depth analytical study of the sharecropping arrangements in the first phase of land reform in Taiwan, in which he shows that when the landlord can specify the amount of labor to be applied, share contracts may be efficient.

Although Cheung's assumption that tenant labor can be perfectly monitored has been severely criticized by many, his approach—to find a rational explanation for the existence of this type of contract—sparked renewed interest in the tenancy question.[3]

Risk sharing and incentives are included in the work of Joseph Stiglitz (1974) and David Newbery (1975) to explain how sharecropping might be an optimal form of contract. Stiglitz, in a principal-agent framework, shows that when labor supply or effort cannot be easily observed, share contracts provide important incentive effects.

Assuming that the landlord is risk neutral, the agent risk averse, and output uncertain, optimal risk sharing could be achieved by paying a fixed wage to the worker. Since the worker's effort is not enforceable, effort would be undersupplied and production would suffer. Maximum incentive for the worker to supply effort would be achieved with a fixed rent for the landlord. This, however, would place the entire risk burden on the worker. Stiglitz shows how the sharecropping solution balances the problems of incentives and risk sharing.

Newbery extends the analysis of Stiglitz and introduces the idea that various forms of tenancy contracts may distinguish between tenants with varying amounts of entrepreneurial skills.

The Interlinkage of Factor Markets

More recently, the literature on agrarian contracts has devoted increasing recognition to the importance of interlinkages in the land, labor, and credit markets for a more complete understanding of agrarian economies. Pranab K. Bardhan, as he reviews the issues of interlocking factor markets, states that

> land reforms in the form of land distribution and intervention in the land market alone cannot be effective if the existing links between land and credit contracts are ignored and a viable alternative to landlords as the major source of credit for small tenants and other peasants is not found. (Bardhan 1980: 82)

Braverman and Srinivasan (1981) use as examples features of agrarian reform laws in India to show how a landlord can nullify the potential benefits of institutional reforms in tenancy (for example, setting legal floors to crop shares) when credit and tenancy are tied under one contract. This follows from their major proposition that in equilibrium all contracts will offer the same utility to the tenant. If the tenant is freed from the landlord, however, and given his own land through a land reform, his utility will increase while production may increase or decrease.

Consumption credit from landlord to tenant is modeled as a device to elicit maximum effort by the tenant in Braverman and Stiglitz (1982). By extending low-interest loans, the landlord can induce the tenant to borrow more. Then to avoid default he must exert more effort to increase production. The model assumes that there are severe penalties for default and that the loan must be paid off at the end of the production period. Finally, it is established that the "utility possibilities frontier" (the potential total utility shared between landlord and tenant) is shifted outward by the interlinking of factor markets.

Ashok Kotwal (1985) points out that this approach by Braverman-Stiglitz does not explain long-lasting indebtedness, since the account must be balanced at harvest. Kotwal explains that

> often, in traditional agriculture, the tenant regards his landlord as a patron who would help him out when the tenant is in difficulty. In bad years the tenant borrows from his landlord, and in good years the landlord demands at least a partial repayment. The amount borrowed fluctuates from year to year, and the debts span not only production periods but lifetimes. (Kotwal 1985: 275)

He then abstracts entirely from the possibility of default and models credit as a side payment that may be positive in bad years when the tenant borrows and negative in good years as he pays back the loan. In the context of a principal-agent model, Kotwal shows that risk can be shifted from a risk-averse tenant to a risk-neutral landlord while maintaining the tenant's incentive to work.

He does this by assuming that output is a separable function of the tenant's effort and some random variable and, further, that the landlord is able to gauge the random fluctuation in output ex-post. This random component is then the side payment that, in combination with a fixed rent, induces the tenant to choose the optimal effort level.

THE DECOLLECTIVIZATION OF AGRICULTURE IN PERU AND THE DOMINICAN REPUBLIC

Although very little microtheoretic literature exists on land reform issues in Latin America, some interesting studies have been undertaken by Michael Carter that focus on the decollectivization of agrarian reform projects in Peru and the Dominican Republic. Along with an empirical study that reveals a wide diversity in the performance of collective farms in coastal Peru (Carter 1984b), he has an insightful theoretical paper (Carter 1987) dealing with exactly the issue we wish to study (that is, the choice among collective farming, individual parcels, and an intermediate solution) based on the experience of the breakdown of collective farms in Peru and the Dominican Republic.

In "Risk Sharing and Incentives in the Decollectivization of Agriculture," Carter first demonstrates in the context of a noncooperative Cournot-Nash game that collective production with equal division of output will yield suboptimal effort levels. Summarizing, Carter states, "The individual behaves socially suboptimally either to free ride, or to avoid being free ridden upon" (Carter 1987: 583).

He then illustrates the trade-off between risk sharing and incentives for the collective, individual, and intermediate solution with the help of a principal-agent model and the previously developed Cournot-Nash equilibrium concept. To look at the choice between institutional alternatives, a linear payment-rule is used where payment to the agent is equal to some fixed (risk-free) component (α) plus a share (β) of his random production (q): thus payment $\equiv y = \alpha + \beta q$.[4]

When $\beta = 0$, the coll1ective situation is represented: Individual payment depends not on individual production but on an equal share of total production. In this case there is complete risk insurance for the individuals in the collective.[5] The parcellation solution is represented by $\beta = 1$: Here, individual payment depends only on individual production such that the incentive effect is maximum but there is no insurance against risk. Carter shows that with risk-averse agents who choose their own effort levels to maximize individual utility, in the optimal payment rule $0 < \beta < 1$. In other words, an intermediate institutional form dominates both the individual and collective solution.

Carter deals only with bilateral contracts between beneficiaries or agents and the collective farm as a unified principal. He does not develop the role of the administrator either as a supervisor or as providing managerial skill.

CONCLUSION

Undeniably the researcher interested in contracts in agriculture has a wide resource base in microeconomic theory from which to draw. The principal-agent literature thoroughly explores the problems of incentives and risk sharing for two parties dividing an observed output. Team theory analyzes the structure of decision making and information within a firm. The literature on hierarchies focuses on the role of supervision in large organizations. Much could be learned from application of these analytical tools to problems of organization in agriculture.

Likewise, literature based on experience in the eastern hemisphere is rich with insights for the microtheorist working on agriculture in Latin America. Studies of the Soviet Union and China illuminate problems of collective enterprise. Studies of India and Southeast Asia have struggled to explain the various existing tenancy contracts and more recently their ties with credit contracts. Certainly there is room to develop a similar literature on the problems of organization in agriculture in Latin America.

Rather than begin, however, by applying models developed for other cultural and institutional environments to the organizational problems of land reform projects in the Dominican Republic, the present study will, in the following chapter, develop a simple, original model including exactly those elements we have shown to be essential in the Dominican case. To repeat, these elements are (1) the crucial role of credit for the small farmer to provide liquidity and to mitigate risk, (2) the potential scale benefits to collectivization, (3) the inevitable free-rider problem with collectivization, (4) the key position of the agrarian reform agency administrator or local leader, and (5) the potential conflict of interest or divergence in incentives between the beneficiaries, administrator or local leader, and the government agency in charge.

Although the principal-agent problem explores the problems involved in bilateral contracts, our problem involves at least three parties: the beneficiary, the administrator or local leader, and the government agency. Team theory assumes that members have a common goal, while agrarian reform beneficiaries in Latin America have shown themselves to be quite individualistic in their orientations. Hierarchy theory limits successive levels of management to the role of supervision without allowing for input of effort into production by these supervisors. In our framework, the administrator plays an essential role in production.

Finally, the tenancy literature of India and Southeast Asia involves strictly bilateral contracts with respect to issues especially relevant for that area; whereas, the studies of socialist collective enterprise are even more limited to the specific conditions of their particular economic framework. Carter's work on Peru and the Dominican Republic analyzes similar issues to those we wish to pursue, but it also neglects the role of the administrator.

In what follows, a model is developed to deal with risk sharing and incentives between three parties when output may not be observable in an associative form of organization intermediate to the collective and individual forms. It is then shown under what conditions this associative enterprise may capture scale benefits, distribute risk, and provide incentives to pareto dominate both the individual and collective forms of organization.

NOTES

1. For a concise characterization of the basic model of team theory see Arrow 1985.

2. Williamson defines this parameter to be the "fraction of work done by a subordinate that contributes to the objectives of his superior" (Williamson 1967: 128).

3. See Quibria and Rashid 1984, or Basu 1984, for a survey of tenancy literature.

4. This type of linear payment-rule to study institutional choice is standard in the tenancy literature (Stiglitz 1974; Kotwal 1985).

5. In order to provide complete risk insurance, Carter assumes that the collective is large enough to self-ensure against microenvironmental risk. He does not take into account more general risk factors such as price and major weather problems that may affect production and cannot be locally insured against.

5

A Hierarchy Model of Associative Farming

The experience of Latin America with land reforms yields a variety of management models of reform projects and considerable wisdom as to the advantages and disadvantages of the alternative forms. Poor results of the agrarian reform in Bolivia are blamed on lack of supporting services for the individual beneficiaries that received land. Mexico has had extensive experience with collective and semi-collective management under the *ejidos*, with mixed reviews as to the success of the reform in general. The massive collective farms set up in Peru under the Velasco military government very rapidly broke down when Belaúnde returned to power.

Economists in agricultural development point out the potential advantages to cooperative effort: easier accessibility to credit opportunities and support services, economies of scale in production, increased bargaining power, as well as better prices and lower transaction costs in purchasing and marketing. The problems with cooperative farming, however, are not to be overlooked. The consensus finds these problems to be focused on internal organization and individual incentive (Barraclough 1976; Dorner and Kanel 1977). The most severe drawback to collective farming is the difficulty of enforcing optimal effort by all. It is also pointed out that the objectives of the government agencies, managers, and beneficiaries usually do not coincide and that the manager plays a particularly key role in the success of a land reform project. Many suggest management models intermediate to the standard collective and individual forms to capture the benefits of both extremes (Schiller 1969; Warriner 1973; Carter 1987).

In the Dominican Republic an attempt has been made by agrarian reform beneficiaries to find their own intermediate solution to the problem of organization. Within the rice sector, land had been appropriated to individual beneficiaries as well as to collective units. Interestingly, many of the individual beneficiaries have associated themselves in order to obtain group credit, purchase inputs and market their rice collectively, and share the cost of capital equipment. At the same time collectives have divided their land into individual parcels and have insisted that the government legalize their associative management structure.

This chapter illustrates the potential advantages of such an associative organizational structure, which captures benefits to group effort while retaining individual initiative, over both the collective and the individual forms.

Kotwal (1985), in the context of a landlord-tenant contract, models consumption credit as a side payment that may be positive in bad years when the tenant borrows and negative in good years when he pays back the loan. Essentially, the continual availability of credit provides insurance against risk in a setting where peasants may remain indebted to their patrons for generations and the possibility of default is not considered.

A similar idea is used here; but instead of a two-party principal-agent model, included is a three-party model consisting of the government agency in charge of administrating the agrarian reform, the local agency administrator, and the agrarian reform beneficiary. Since both the beneficiary and the administrator provide effort for production, the incentive problem of each must be dealt with. In doing so, the administrator is treated quite differently than are the supervisors of standard hierarchy theory (Williamson 1967; Stiglitz 1975; Mirrlees 1976), who provide no real input to production.

Carter (1987) demonstrates in the framework of a noncooperative Cournot-Nash game that collective production with equal division of output will yield suboptimal effort levels. The same Cournot-Nash equilibrium concept is employed here, adapted to show the suboptimality of the collective form relative to the associative model.

First a general model of an agrarian reform project is set up. Next, an associative farming model is developed in a three-person principal-agent hierarchy where both the beneficiary and the agency administrator supply effort and are risk averse. Credit, in the form of side payments, shifts risk to a risk-neutral third party—the government agency. The associative model is then contrasted to a collective model where, although scale benefits may be captured, a Cournot-Nash game yields suboptimal effort levels on the part of the beneficiaries. Following this, the equilibrium of the associative model is contrasted to that of the individual model, where the agency administrator contributes no effort and credit in the form of side payments is not available. Finally, to conclude the chapter, an alternative structure of associative farming is presented.

A GENERAL MODEL OF AN AGRARIAN REFORM PROJECT

The Basic Model

The basic model involves essentially three parties: the government agency in charge of the land reform, an agency administrator, and the land reform beneficiary.

The beneficiary produces an agricultural output that is a function of his own effort, e_1, the administrator's effort, e_2, and some random element, θ, which may include the effects of weather as well as other unanticipated factors—such as the health of the beneficiary and his family—that influence agricultural production. I abstract from other production inputs to focus on the problem of incentives.[1] For simplicity, this function is assumed to be separable between effort levels and the random element as follows:[2]

$$y = y(e_1, e_2,) = x(e_1, e_2) + \theta$$

Output, x, is increasing in effort levels and strictly concave and so yields a convex production set that can be uniquely maximized. The effort levels of the beneficiary and administrator are complementary inputs, $x_{12} > 0$, and there are assumed to be no fixed costs, that is, $x(0,0) = 0$. Finally, the random element, θ, has a mean of zero and a distribution that is common knowledge.

The agricultural production by the joint efforts of the beneficiary and the administrator is the only production that occurs; and since it may be in part consumed by the beneficiary's household, it is directly observable by the beneficiary alone. The administrator is entitled to some share of the production because of his input of effort. The government agency provides a service of credit (to be described in what follows) and holds definitive title to the land. As a consequence, the government agency is entitled to some share as well.

Although the focus here is on the relationships among the beneficiary, the administrator, and the agrarian reform agency, the total number of persons involved is not ignored. I assume a fixed number, m, of identical administrators, and for each administrator, a fixed number, n, of identical beneficiaries. Total production, then, is defined to be the sum of all $m \cdot n$ beneficiaries' production. Since beneficiaries and administrators are identical, this will be simply $m \cdot n$ times the production of one beneficiary plus the sum of all random components:

$$m \cdot nx(e_1,e_2) \; + \; \sum_{i=1}^{m \cdot n} \theta_i$$

In making this assumption I am saying that there are no economies of scale in production. I have assumed, as does Carter (1987), that the joint production of the beneficiaries is no more that the sum of their individual production, such that the scale of production is the same whether on $m \cdot n$ individual parcels or m collective farms engaging in joint production.

Here, the potential benefits to association are captured by the effort level of the administrator. This is a reasonable representation of rice production in the reform sector of the Dominican Republic but can certainly not be generalized to all other crops and situations. Earlier I described the key role of the local leader or administrator as a liaison in the obtaining of credit, purchasing inputs, and rice marketing. Hence the major gains to be had from cooperative effort in this situation depend on the behavior of this representative rather than the larger scale, per se, of production.

The government agency is assumed to be risk neutral[3] and thus interested in the maximization of production net wages of the administrators and beneficiaries.

The land reform beneficiary and the agency administrator have utility functions defined over income, ϕ_i, and effort, e_i, which for simplicity are assumed to be separable:

$$W_k(\phi_k,e_k) = U_k(\phi_k) - V_k(e_k) \quad \text{for } k = 1,2$$

referring to the beneficiary and the administrator respectively. Both are risk averse with positive and diminishing marginal utility of income, $U_k' > 0$, $U_k'' < 0$, and positive and increasing disutility of effort, $V_k' > 0$, $V_k'' > 0$.

The problem, from the point of view of the government agency, is to design a "contract" that optimally distributes risk and provides the proper incentives, to both beneficiary and administrator, for efficient production.

The "First-Best" Problem

It is standard in the contract literature to look at the case of perfect information, called the first-best problem, as a point of comparison. Assume, as is also standard, that the agency designing the contract must offer a contract or effort-wage combination that provides utility equal to or greater than some minimum utility level, that is, $W_1°$, $W_2°$, for the beneficiary and administrator respectively.

With full information of output level, production, and utility functions, and with perfect observation and enforcement of effort levels, the government agency could maximize expected agency utility by choosing effort levels and wages for the beneficiary and administrator, subject to minimum utility levels for each. By paying wages, the agency would absorb all the risk involved in the random output and so achieve an optimal distribution of risk. The problem is formulated thus:

$$(1) \; \underset{e_1,e_2,\phi_1,\phi_2}{\text{Max}} \; E[m \cdot nx(e_1,e_2) + \sum_{i=1}^{m \cdot n} \theta_i - m \cdot n\phi_1 - m\phi_2], \quad \text{s.t.}$$

$$(1.1) \quad U_1(\phi_1) - V_1(e_1) = W_1{}^\circ$$

$$(1.2) \quad U_2(\phi_2) - V_2(e_2) = W_2{}^\circ$$

The first-order conditions for this problem are as follows:

$$(1.3) \quad U_1'(\phi_1)x_1(e_1,e_2) = V_1'(e_1)$$

$$(1.4) \quad U_2'(\phi_2)x_2(e_1,e_2) = V_2'(e_2)/n$$

These have the interpretation that for the beneficiary, the product of the marginal utility of income and the marginal product of effort is equal to the marginal disutility of effort. For the administrator, the same is equal to his marginal disutility of work divided over n beneficiaries. Conditions (1.3) and (1.4) combined with the minimum utility restrictions can be solved for the first-best solution denoted $e_1{}^*,e_2{}^*,\phi_1{}^*,\phi_2{}^*$.

AN EFFICIENT CONTRACT WITH IMPERFECT INFORMATION

It is unreasonable to assume, however, that the government agency can perfectly observe and enforce the effort level of the administrator, much less that of the beneficiary. Nor would the agency be able to observe output, since part of the production could very well be consumed by the beneficiary's household before either the administrator or the head office could quantify it.

One could reasonably assume that the agency has knowledge of the production function, as well as the utility functions of the beneficiary and the administrator. With such minimal information, can a contract be designed to provide proper incentives and distribute risk?

The literature on landlord-tenant relationships reveals that for bilateral contracts, when effort is not enforceable, a rent contract will yield optimal results by providing maximum incentive if the tenant is risk neutral. Kotwal (1985) shows that when the tenant is risk averse, a rent contract in combination with side payments of credit to shift the risk to the risk-neutral landlord yield a first-best solution. I will first show this in a significantly modified version of Kotwal's landlord-tenant model. Then, for the associative farming model, I will show that a hierarchical rent contract—that is, where the beneficiary pays a rent or quota to the administrator, who in turn pays a quota to the government agency—in combination with a similar credit mechanism can also yield a first-best solution.

The Landlord-Tenant Case

To examine first the simplest case, reduce the model to two parties, a landlord and tenant (where the landlord now takes the position of the government agency, the administrator is dropped, and the tenant may be thought of as the beneficiary), so that production is a separable function of the tenant's effort and some random variable:

$$y(e,\theta) = x(e) + \theta$$

Make all the corresponding assumptions to those made before, dropping subscripts since there is only a tenant, rather than both beneficiary and administrator.

In the first-best problem, with full information and the ability to enforce the effort level of the tenant, the risk-neutral landlord maximizes expected income by choosing an effort level and a wage for the tenant, subject to the tenant's minimum utility condition, and absorbing all risk:

(2) Max $E(x(e) + \theta - \phi)$, s.t.
ϕ,e

(2.1) $U(\phi) - V(e) = W^\circ$

Taking first-order conditions, (2.2), will yield the marginal condition we found earlier for the beneficiary, that is, that the product of the marginal utility of income and the marginal product of effort is equal to the marginal disutility of effort:

(2.2) $U'(\phi)x'(e) = V'(e)$

Solving equations (2.1) and (2.2) yields the first-best optimal solution e^*,ϕ^*.

Under the more reasonable assumption that the effort level of the tenant may not be observed and that the landlord has knowledge of the tenant's utility and production function but not the output level,[4] the landlord would be unable to collect output and pay a fee to achieve this first-best solution. He would, however, be able to decide on a rent level or quota. If one assumes, as does Kotwal, that the landlord can perfectly observe the random component of production, θ, ex-post, and compensate the tenant for it with credit—a positive payment in bad years and a negative payment in good years—this side payment in combination with a fixed rent will yield the first best solution.

The following proposition is a reformulation of Kotwal's result:

Proposition 1: A landlord will optimally provide incentives and distribute risk in a tenancy contract by setting total rent, R, equal to some fixed quota plus a side payment that is random. The fixed quota, Q^q, should be equal to the income the landlord would receive in the first best contract, $x(e^*) - \phi^*$, and the side payment should be set equal to θ, the variation in output due to unanticipated factors. That is, $R = Q^q + \theta$.

Intuitively, the incentive problem is resolved because both the land-lord and tenant have the same goal—to maximize production: the land-lord so that he can take the largest quota possible, and the tenant because he can keep all the excess after he pays the quota. The assumption that $y(e,\theta)$ is separable in effort and the random variable allows the risk to be shifted entirely to the risk-neutral party. Although it may seem odd that while the landlord does not observe total output, he does observe the random component, the effects of adverse weather or an illness of the beneficiary may in fact be far more visible that total output.

Proposition 1 will now be demonstrated in two steps: First shown will be that under an agreement to make compensation for random output, the landlord will choose $Q^q = x(e^*) - \phi^*$; and then that the tenant will respond by choosing e^*.

The landlord seeks to maximize expected rent subject to the minimum utility of the tenant:[5]

(3) Max $E(Q + \theta)$, s.t.
$\quad e,Q$

(3.1) $U(x(e) + \theta - (Q + \theta)) - V(e) = W^\circ$

Note that the tenant's income will consist of the value of production, $x(e) + \theta$, minus a fixed quota and compensation for the randomness in output, $Q + \theta$.

The first-order conditions to this problem yield the marginal condition:

(3.2) $U'(x(e) - Q)x'(e) = V'(e)$

Solving equations (3.1) and (3.2) yields the solution e^q, Q^q, where $e^q = e^*$ and $Q^q = x(e^*) - \phi^*$.

This should not be stated without proof, but the proof is trivial: It is true that e^*, Q^* satisfy the conditions (2.1) and (2.2); therefore e^q, Q^q, as defined, satisfy conditions (3.1) and (3.2). Since the solution is unique in both problems, it must be the case that $e^q = e^*$ and $Q^q = x(e^*) - \phi^*$.

Since it has *not* been assumed that the landlord can enforce the effort level, one must look at how the tenant responds to Q^q. When the tenant is faced with a certain quota to pay and is promised compensation for the random output, the tenant will maximize as follows:

$$\text{Max}_{e} \quad U(x(e) + \theta - (Q^q + \theta)) - V(e)$$

with first-order condition

$$U'(x(e) - Q^q) \, x'(e) = V'(e)$$

Because the tenant's first-order condition coincides with (3.2) of the landlord's problem, given Q^q, he must choose $e^q = e^*$. When the tenant chooses e^*, his income is $x(e^*) - Q^q = \phi^*$ and the landlord's income is $Q^q + \theta = x(e^*) - \phi^* + \theta$, exactly as in the first-best case.

The Associative Farming Case

Returning to the model of an agrarian reform project under imperfect information, I will now show that a similar credit mechanism combined with a hierarchical rent contract will yield first-best results in a model of associative farming.

A hierarchical rent contract is used to refer to the age-old system by which the head of a hierarchy can maximize his return by requiring a quota from each of his subordinates, who in turn requires a quota from those subordinate to him, and so on down to the lowest level of the hierarchy. This arrangement has been used for thousands of years in feudal contracts, where output is random, effort levels are not enforceable, and production takes place at the lowest level of the hierarchy. In the Dominican Republic, a similar system is firmly in place among corrupt officials taking bribes, each owing a quota to his superior. Of course, I advocate neither corruption nor a return to feudalism. Simply, what must be noted is that the mechanism does seem to provide a way for a hierarchy, that has the authority to require payment—though it is powerless to enforce effort, to maximize production. Theoretically interesting under a multitude of situations, the hierarchical rent contract is analyzed here only in terms of an associative farming model.

As mentioned earlier, the hierarchical rent contract will be combined with a credit mechanism to achieve first-best results. This latter deserves some comment as well. To shift risk to the risk-neutral government agency, I make the assumption that the administrator observes θ_i, the random component of production, for each of the n beneficiaries he supervises and truthfully reports it to the land reform agency. The agency is under agreement to compensate the beneficiary for this random component, giving loans in bad years and collecting payment in good years.

Admittedly this mechanism is a bit ad hoc (even as it is in Kotwal's formulation) and merits justification. In the first place, making the assumption allows me to illustrate theoretically, in an easily understood manner, that an associative can provide credit to relieve the risk burden on land reform beneficiaries, when from observation it is known that associatives, as well as collectives, do serve this function. As demonstrated in earlier chapters, the provision of credit—for production and inevitably consumption—to the land reform beneficiary, and the recuperation of that credit, is perhaps the most difficult and complex problem facing the agrarian reform agency. I am not attempting to solve that problem with this model. For this reason the intricate problems of supply and demand of funds or default are not treated here.

As argued in the landlord-tenant case, the effects of weather on a beneficiary's plot of land can be determined by casual observation as the administrator goes about his ordinary daily activities, involving contact with each of the beneficiaries. Likewise, word of misfortune—health problems in the family, for instance—or good luck, such as particularly high yields, travels quickly in a small community and would easily be brought to the attention of the administrator. Although it may seem that there might be incentives for the administrator to misrepresent θ, the beneficiary also observes θ and in practice both beneficiary and administrator would sign the loan papers. Since the beneficiary is held liable to pay back in the future all loans he makes (in the long run the sum of θ for each beneficiary over many periods should approach zero), he would not want to mount up loans unnecessarily. Furthermore, since the mean of θ is equal to zero, the sum of θ_i over all n beneficiaries in the land reform project should be close to zero such that any administrator continually reporting losses would be brought under suspicion.

Consider the following proposition:

Proposition 2: A land reform agency will optimally provide incentives and distribute risk in an associative farming model, with a hierarchical rent contract, by setting some fixed quota, $Q_2{}^q$, equal to the income per administrator the agency would receive in the first-best contract, $nx(e_1{}^*, e_2{}^*) - n\phi_1{}^* - \phi_2{}^*$, and collecting side payments equal to the variation in output due to unanticipated factors. Consequently the agency receives:

$$Q_2{}^q + \sum_{i=1}^{n}\theta_i$$

from each administrator.

The proof for this proposition proceeds exactly as in the landlord-tenant case. First shown is that under the aforementioned credit mechanism, the agency will choose $Q_2{}^q$ to collect from each administrator equal to the income per administrator that would be received in the first-best case. Then it is shown that the administrator will respond by setting a quota per beneficiary, $Q_1{}^q$, such that his income, $nQ_1{}^q - Q_2{}^q$, as well as his chosen effort level, will be the same as in the first-best case. Finally, it is shown that the beneficiary also responds by choosing an effort level equal to that in the first-best case. The proof can be found in the Appendix.

To achieve this first-best solution, I have assumed that the agency knows only the production function and the utility functions of the beneficiary and the administrator but that he cannot observe or enforce effort levels. Likewise I have assumed that the administrator knows the production function and the utility function of the beneficiary but that he cannot observe or enforce the beneficiary's effort. Neither the agency nor the administrator observes total output.

As in the landlord-tenant case, the contract is self-enforcing because all parties involved are interested in the maximization of production: the agency and administrator in order to be able to require larger quotas, and the beneficiary because all production in excess of the quota he pays the administrator belongs to him.

The model, clearly, is an abstraction. It represents neither exactly how the associatives function in the Dominican Republic nor how any specific land reform project in Latin America should be organized. What it provides is an illustration of the potential of the associative form. When each beneficiary keeps the produce from his plot of land, when the benefits to cooperative effort are captured by effective leadership, when credit is provided to relieve the burden of risk on the land reform beneficiary, efficient production can, in fact, be achieved. As described in an earlier chapter, the associatives in the Dominican Republic function in a variety of ways. The beneficiaries receive their own production, credit is obtained from a government agency, and collective advantages (in those associatives that are successful) are gained by the efforts of enthusiastic local leaders. This model provides, rather, a structure that can be imposed from above, for in general, this is how agrarian reform is handled in the initial stages.

The agency administrator initially assumes a very important role in the success of the land reform project. Although it is hardly necessary to demonstrate that effort will be underprovided by an administrator who receives a fixed wage when his effort level is not observable, this is easily done in the context of this model. The administrator would choose e_2 to maximize his utility where $\phi_2{}^\circ$ is his fixed wage:

$$\text{Max}_{e_2} \ U_2(\phi_2{}^\circ) - V_2(e_2)$$

and obtain the first order condition

$$V_2{}'(e_2) = 0$$

Since marginal disutility is positive for all positive values of e_2, for this condition to hold, he would apply no effort. It is thus demonstrated that if the administrator is to carry out his intended role, his income must depend on the agricultural production.

I will now compare this associative model to the collective and individual project models and finally conclude by discussing an associative farming structure that need not be imposed from above.

THE ASSOCIATIVE AND COLLECTIVE MODELS CONTRASTED

In reviewing the agrarian reform projects in the Dominican Republic, the essential difference in organization between collectives and associatives was found to be that of how profits are divided. In the collectives, the total profit is basically divided equally among members; whereas in the associatives, each is responsible for his own costs and production. The central role of the agrarian reform agency is to provide credit in both cases. Local leadership and/or agency administrators play the role of liaison for credit, marketing, and input purchases. Thus the collective is here modeled exactly as the associative except for this major difference in the division of profits.

Production in the collective is defined, as presented earlier in the general model of a reform project, as the sum of all beneficiaries' production. In defining production in this way I have not allowed for economies of scale in production on the collective but only consider those potential benefits to collective organization as the same that could be gained by the associative form. As observed, in practice both collectives and associatives face similar problems with respect to the administrative structure that captures the advantages of group effort. Certainly the salaried government administrator would have no more incentive to provide effort on a collective farm than on an associative farm, if one assumes in both cases that administrator effort levels are not observable to the government agency.

Recognizing the comparability of the incentive problems of the administrator in the two cases, I make the comparison of the collective to the associative under conditions where the collective has equal potential to provide the group benefits. For this reason the collective is modeled like the associative before, in a setting where the government agency chooses a quota for the administrator, who in turn chooses a quota for the group of beneficiaries. Likewise the same credit mechanism is used. Thus, optimal incentives are provided for the administrator, the risk burden is removed from the beneficiary, and the focus is exclusively on the question of division of profits.

Consider the following proposition:

Proposition 3: Under the collective form of organization, even when the administrator is provided with proper incentives and credit relieves the risk burden on beneficiaries, the effort choice among the beneficiaries results in a low-productivity solution.

The proof of the Proposition 3 proceeds in a similar manner to that of Proposition 2. First, it is shown that the agency will choose a quota, $Q_2{}^c$, to collect from each administrator equal to the income per reform project that would be received in the first-best case. Then it is shown that the administrator will respond by setting a quota for the collective, $Q_1{}^c$, such that his income, $Q_1{}^c - Q_2{}^c$, as well as his chosen effort level, will be the same as in the first-best case. However, when it comes time for the beneficiary to choose his effort level, it is shown that since he receives only $1/n$ th of the marginal benefit to his effort, his effort level will be less than optimal. The complete proof can be found in the Appendix, but I include next a discussion of the beneficiary's effort decision.

Total profit from the point of view of any one beneficiary is equal to his production plus everyone else's production minus the quota to be paid to the administrator; and his share is $1/n$ th of this total. When the collective is provided credit to relieve the burden of risk, and demanded the quota, $Q_1{}^c$, by the administrator, then the maximization problem of beneficiary i is as follows:

$$\underset{e_{1i}}{\text{Max}}\ U_{1i}[(1/n)(x(e_{1i},e_2{}^c) + \sum_{j\neq i}^{n} x(e_{1j},e_2{}^c) - Q_1{}^c)] - V_{1i}(e_{1i})$$

Taking the partial derivative with respect to e_{1i} yields the first-order condition:

$$(1/n)U_{1i}{}'[(1/n)(x(e_{1i},e_2{}^c) + \sum_{j\neq i}^{n} x(e_{1j},e_2{}^c) - Q_1{}^c)]x_1(e_{1i},e_2{}^c) = V_{1i}{}'(e_{1i})$$

This has the interpretation that for the beneficiary, $1/n$ times the marginal utility of the marginal product of effort (that is, $1/n$ times the marginal benefit of effort) is equated to the marginal disutility of effort.

Note that the beneficiary's decision depends upon how much he believes the others will produce, which, following Carter's notation, I will call z:

$$z \equiv \sum_{j\neq i}^{n} x(e_{1j},e_2{}^c)$$

Marginal utility of income falls as z rises, which implies that if the beneficiary believes that the others are working a lot, he will work less or free ride. But if he works less and all behave the same way, everyone will be working less and the realized value of other's production will not correspond to his belief about the value of z. In this case, the beneficiary would have to adjust his belief and his effort decision. For a Cournot-Nash equilibrium, the beneficiary's conjecture about the value of the other's production must be consistent with what occurs, so that there is no need for further adjustment.

Since all beneficiaries are identical, in equilibrium all must choose the same effort level, $e_{1i} = e_1{}^N$, for all i and

$$(1/n)U_1{}'[(1/n)(nx(e_1{}^N,e_2{}^c) - Q_1{}^c)]x_1(e_1{}^N,e_2{}^c) = V_1{}'(e_1{}^N)$$

Figure 5.1 illustrates that this equilibrium value of effort, $e_1{}^N$, must be strictly less that the first-best level. The marginal disutility of effort is strictly increasing and the marginal benefit of effort is strictly decreasing. For the first-best solution they are set equal at $e_1{}^*$. At the Cournot-Nash noncooperative equilibrium, $1/n$ times the marginal benefit of effort is set equal to its marginality disutility, which results in a less than optimal level of effort, $e_1{}^N$.

Unless the beneficiaries are motivated by noneconomic goals, or include the long-term good of the collective in their utility function, one would not expect to achieve as much productivity under the collective form of organization as under an associative form where the same benefits to cooperative effort are available but each beneficiary is responsible for his own costs and production. This is not to say that there are no beneficiaries farsighted enough to behave in a manner that will achieve other than this low-effort, noncooperative outcome. The experience in the Dominican Republic would suggest, however, that they are few—that in fact most of the beneficiaries would like to see the full marginal benefit to their effort in the short run—hence the breakdown of the collectives. Those that are farsighted have become the local leaders and are among the fiercest supporters of the associative form of organization.

THE ASSOCIATIVE AND INDIVIDUAL MODELS CONTRASTED

In the Dominican Republic, as well as Latin America in general, agrarian reform projects in which land is allocated in small parcels to individuals are characterized by lack of agency support for purposes of credit and other services. Each beneficiary must do his own marketing and purchase his own inputs, not only facing prices less desirable than those that could be obtained by a larger producer or an association of small producers, but also having to incur all of the transaction costs involved himself. This section demonstrates in terms of the general model the relative inefficiency of the individual model to the optimal results obtained in the associative model.

Figure 5.1
Cournot–Nash Equilibrium

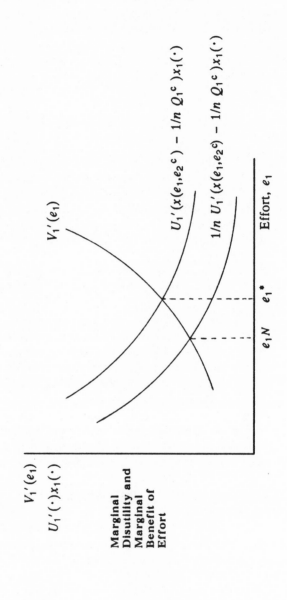

Since neither credit nor services of an administrator are provided, the focus here is on the maximization problem of the beneficiary. The production function is the same as in the general case:

$$y = y(e_1, e_2, \theta) = x(e_1, e_2) + \theta$$

except that producing as an individual, the effort level of the administrator is equal to zero, $e_2 = 0$. Without access to credit to remove the burden of risk, the beneficiary chooses his effort level to maximize the expected utility of his income minus the disutility of effort:

$$\underset{e_1}{\text{Max }} EU_1(x(e_1, 0) + \theta) - V_1(e_1)$$

Taking the partial derivative with respect to e_1 yields the first-order condition,

$$EU_1'(x(e_1, 0) + \theta)x_1(e_1, 0) = V_1(e_1)$$

and the solution, denoted $e_1{}^P$.

I demonstrate efficiency loss on two accounts: (1) lack of accessibility to the benefits that could be provided by an agency administrator or the leaders of an association and (2) lack of accessibility to credit to relieve the burden of risk. The following proposition addresses itself to the former of these two.

Proposition 4: When individual land reform beneficiaries produce without the effort of an administrator to capture group benefits, a deadweight loss to society results by the amount of the wages the beneficiaries would be willing to pay to receive such effort.

This proposition can be shown very simply by recognizing that at the beneficiary's choice of effort under individual production, $e_1{}^P$, more production could be obtained with the services of an administrator. That is,

$$x(e_1{}^P, e_2) > x(e_1{}^P, 0) \text{ for all } e_2 > 0$$

Therefore, for some particular level of effort, $\hat{e}_2$, there exists some wage or fee, $\hat{\phi}_2$, such that

$$x(e_1{}^P, \hat{e}_2) - \hat{\phi}_2 = x(e_1{}^P, 0)$$

With that the case, the beneficiary could achieve a utility level equal to his maximum utility under individual production by employing those services and paying a fee,

$$EU_1(x(e_1{}^P, \hat{e}_2) + \theta - \hat{\phi}_2) - V_1(e_1{}^P) = EU_1(x(e_1{}^P, 0) + \theta) - V_1(e_1{}^P)$$

if the services were available at a fee he could afford.

There are, however, large economies of scale in the provision of e_2. It has been assumed that an administrator can provide his effort to n beneficiaries at the same cost as he can provide it to an individual. This assumption is supported by agrarian reform agency administrators who have attempted to work with both individual and associatives or collectives in the Dominican Republic.[6] Without $n - 1$ other beneficiaries to help him pay an administrator, a single individual would not have access to these services. That amount, $\hat{\phi}_2$, that he would be willing to pay for such service were it available represents a deadweight loss to society.

With a similar line of argument, I address the problem of lack of accessibility to credit in the following proposition:

Proposition 5: When risk averse beneficiaries engage in production and receive a random output for their efforts, a deadweight loss to society results by the amount they would be willing to pay to eliminate the risk.

To demonstrate this proposition, the concept of the risk premium must be defined. The risk premium is defined over some particular income level and some risk. In this case the income level would be output at some particular effort level $x(\hat{e}_1,0)$ and the risk, θ. Then the risk premium $\pi(x(\hat{e}_1,0),\theta)$ is defined such that for any $x(\hat{e}_1,0)$ and risk θ, one would be indifferent between receiving the risk θ and the nonrandom

$$E(\theta) - \pi(x(\hat{e}_1,0), \theta)$$

For the risk-averse individual, the risk premium is positive. Since $E(\theta) = 0$, this implies that

$$EU(x(\hat{e}_1,0) + \theta) = U[x(\hat{e}_1,0) - \pi(x(\hat{e}_1,0), \theta)]$$

Therefore, by the definition of the risk premium, at the effort level $e_1{}^P$, for the risk-averse individual beneficiary there exists some positive amount $\pi(x(e_1{}^P,0),\theta)$ such that

$$EU(x(e_1{}^P,0) + \theta) = U[x(e_1{}^P,0) - \pi(x(e_1{}^P,0), \theta)]$$

This means that at certain income level $x(e_1{}^P,0)$, the risk-averse beneficiary would be willing to pay the amount $\pi(x(e_1{}^P,0),\theta)$ to be free of the risk involved in θ. Consequently, there is a deadweight loss to society by the amount of the risk premium.

Because for each beneficiary there is a loss in efficiency due to the lack of advantages that could be provided by an administrator and the lack of accessibility to credit, certainly gains in efficiency could be had by associating to hire an administrator (or administrative council) and to obtain group credit. In fact, this has occurred in a number of cases in the rice sector in the Dominican Republic. The change from the individual form to the associative is not automatic, however. Large fixed costs for the group of beneficiaries are involved in setting up an administrative structure. The supply of administrators is not perfectly elastic, and someone has to take the initiative to get the group together. Yet, as is not difficult to see, once these initial costs are overcome, there are gains to be made by forming an association.

AN ALTERNATIVE ASSOCIATIVE STRUCTURE

This chapter began by developing a model of associative organization that could be imposed by an agrarian reform agency; it now concludes by developing a model of individual beneficiaries who associate, hire an administrator, and pay for the provision of credit.

It should be noted that to speak in terms of "hiring an administrator" is abstracting to a large extent from what has been observed in the Dominican Republic. But it is necessary to make this abstraction, since what is observed is a different administrative structure in each case, and this structure depends in large part on the human resources available and the personalities involved. In some cases, the president of the association may bear most of the responsibility for the activities included under e_2, while receiving only intangible rewards, such as personal recognition and social status, that come along with such a role. In other cases, there may be someone in charge of marketing, another who takes the leadership role of president and representative to outside agencies, and a third who is treasurer, each receiving a wage. The common characteristic, however, is that in general there is some type of compensation, tangible or intangible, from the beneficiaries to the administrator, for his administrative effort.

The following proposition is made:

Proposition 6: Risk-averse individual beneficiaries can associate and, by paying a fee to an administrator or local leader and to an agency willing to assume the risk, can achieve efficiency in production.

As an illustration of this final proposition, consider the maximization problem for the individual beneficiary. His income is now equal to his own production, $x(e_1, e_2) + \theta$, minus his share of a wage for the administrator and a fee to the credit agency to cover the transaction costs involved in the provision of credit, minus a side payment equal to the random component in production. As before, the administrator may act as the third party, the liaison between the beneficiary and government agency, who confirms what the value of this random side payment should be. Since, as assumed earlier, the beneficiary *can* observe the administrator's effort and hence can refuse payment unless proper effort is applied, he maximizes utility, subject to minimum utility levels for agency and administrator, by choosing his own effort level as well as the administrator's and by choosing the fees, ϕ_2 and ϕ_3, for the administrator and credit agency respectively. Identical beneficiaries would have no problem agreeing on what these choice variables should be. The beneficiary's problem is as follows:

(4) $\underset{e_1, e_2, \phi_2, \phi_3}{\text{Max}} U_1(x(e_1, e_2) + \theta - \phi_2 - \phi_3 - \theta)$,   s.t.

(4.1) $U_2(n\phi_2) - V_2(e_2) = W_2^\circ$

(4.2) $E(n\phi_3 + \sum_{i=1}^{n} \theta_i) = W_3^\circ$

Taking partial derivatives with respect to the choice variables will yield conditions that reduce to the following:

(4.3) $U_1'(x(e_1, e_2) - \phi_2 - \phi_3)x_1(e_1, e_2) = V_1'(e_1)$

(4.4) $U_2'(n\phi_2)x_2(e_1, e_2) = V_2'(e_2)/n$

These are not the same conditions as in the first-best problem, but the difference is only that instead of the agency receiving all the surplus after offering both administrator and beneficiary minimum utility contracts, here the beneficiary receives all the surplus after offering the credit agency and administrator minimum utility contracts. The marginal conditions that for the beneficiary, equate marginal benefit and marginal disutility of effort, and for the administrator equate marginal benefit of effort to marginal disutility divided over n beneficiaries, hold, just as they do in the first-best case.

Thus, it is shown that for efficient associative production, a hierarchical structure of authoritative control is not necessary, but that a group of beneficiaries may together bear the costs of maintaining an administrative structure and obtaining group credit.

CONCLUSION

Theoretical justification is therefore provided for the recent shift in the rice sector in agrarian reform projects in the Dominican Republic to an associative organizational form from both the collective and individual reform project structures. Certainly the problem of the precise structure of the administrative council and the details of how to provide credit adequately and efficiently to a group of agrarian reform beneficiaries have not been fully dealt with here, and further research is still required. What has been accomplished, however, is a demonstration that an agrarian reform agency may impose an efficient organizational project structure instead of leaving the beneficiaries to their own devices or paying a wage to an administrator to oversee a collective project when he has very little incentive to work for the success of the project. Further, it has been shown that it is possible to have an equally efficient structure with the burden of responsibility shifted to the beneficiaries, when, after some years of education under agency administrators, local leaders may arise within the group of beneficiaries to carry out the administrative and leadership tasks.

NOTES

1. Additionally, in this static, partial-equilibrium framework I abstract from the role of technology, the impact of changes in terms of trade, and long-run investment considerations.

2. Kotwal makes a similar assumption on the additive separability of the production function, justifying it on the grounds that in general there is little opportunity to mitigate these unanticipated factors by increased effort such that the cross-partial effects on output between effort levels and may be taken to be zero.

3. Risk neutrality is implied by a linear utility function and means indifference between taking some risk and receiving the expected value of that risk. (Since maximizing a linear function of income is the same as maximizing income, we omit the utility function to avoid notational clutter.) Risk aversion is implied by a concave utility function. The risk-averse individual would prefer to receive, with certainty, the expected value of a gamble rather than take the risk.

4. It should be noted that the assumption that output is not observable is a major difference between this model and much of the standard agency theory.

5. Although the landlord's interest is in choosing only Q, with knowledge of the production function and tenant's utility he will find the optimal effort as well. This is as in the standard principal-agent literature. See, for example, Holmstrom 1979.

6. The rice associatives in the Dominican Republic vary in size from approximately 40 to 70 members.

6

An Evaluation of the Associative Reform Projects in the Dominican Republic

The experience of Latin America with agrarian reform projects, reviewed in Chapter 1, demonstrates the need for careful study of the appropriate organizational structures for the projects, as well as flexibility in responding to the needs of the beneficiaries in each specific case. In the Dominican Republic, beneficiaries in the rice sector have indicated rather dramatically their preference for an intermediate associative reform project structure over either extreme of individual or collective farming. Theoretical justification for the transition to the associative structure was given in the last chapter, under assumptions appropriate to the case in the Dominican Republic. To conclude the study, I would like to evaluate whether that transition has indeed been successful.

In the few years since the passage of the associative law in March of 1985, or even the de facto breakdown of the collectives in 1982 and 1983, it is very difficult to say anything definite about the success of the move. There are some indications, however, that the news is encouraging.

This chapter begins with the positive evaluations of those local leaders active in the transition to the associative structure. A following discussion provides empirical support for the success of the associative structure at both the local and national levels. Then before concluding the study, this chapter focuses briefly on the direction of agrarian reform currently in the Dominican Republic.

A POSITIVE EVALUATION BY LOCAL LEADERS

Without exception, those local leaders interviewed in July of 1987 were very positive about the associative structure of organization.[1]

From those that functioned as collectives, the leaders spoke of the superior opportunity for the individual to work for his own progress while still enjoying the benefits of association. The collective was referred to by Guarín in Santa Clara as a "system of injustice and ignorance" on the part of those who instituted it, a system that had always been unacceptable to the beneficiaries. In the associative, members can participate to the degree they desire in the collective activities of the group.

Likewise, those leaders of associatives of farmers who had been assigned individual rights were very happy with the fruits of their collective efforts. One of the main benefits pointed to, aside from the opportunity for better prices on inputs and the opportunity for group credit, is the process of education that takes place within the group as farmers learn from one another in their efforts to solve problems within the associations. They also felt that as an association they had the power to progress as individuals and as a community.

These more qualitative benefits of the associative are not to overshadow the bottom line, however. Both the ex-collectives and the ex-individual projects reported higher net income under the associative form.

Problems with the associative structure do occur at the administrative level, and these problems include group decision making, credit responsibility, and particularly educating beneficiaries to carry out administrative roles adequately. We have noted earlier that the success of the associative structure depends critically on whether an administrative structure is able to capture the benefits to cooperative action. The agrarian reform projects discussed here have had the advantage of highly motivated local leaders willing to assume the administrative role. The appearance of such men is not automatic, however. In fact, there is wide agreement among IAD personnel and beneficiaries alike that relatively few beneficiaries have the ability to act in this capacity. Nor should it be assumed that leaders should be willing to step in to perform this role without adequate compensation. In this matter the IAD might take the initiative to set-up the associatives in such a way that the administrators are provided with the proper incentives to complete their very important job.

On the other hand, the administrative problems on the associatives are no worse than they were on the collectives. For the collectives as for the associatives, the local leaders and the IAD administrators were the key to success. The associatives do have the advantage, however, of providing incentives to the individual farmers that the collective structure is unable to offer, by making them responsible for their own production.

EMPIRICAL SUPPORT FOR AN ASSOCIATIVE STRUCTURE

Before entering into a discussion of empirical data on productivity and net benefits in the reform sector, it is necessary to point out the degree of skepticism that should be exercised in this endeavor. Individual members may or may not report their production to the group; and when they do report, there is no reason to believe that all of the production is reported. Significant amounts may be kept for home consumption. On a national level, the number of groups that report production year after year varies widely. Additionally, all the various agencies in agriculture in the Dominican Republic collect numbers that bear little resemblance one to another. For these reasons only the most pronounced trends can be taken with any degree of faith.

With that said, however, from the empirical data at this point, at least there is no evidence to show that the move to the associative form has been a mistake. The data on productivity yields (production per hectare) at both the local and national levels indicate that no loss has been suffered in productivity, while some gains have been made, due to the new associative structure.

At the National Level

Over the 25 years of agrarian reform in the Dominican Republic, between 1962 and 1986, the production as well as the consumption of rice increased dramatically. Table 6.1 illustrates the production, imports, and per capita consumption of rice over the period.

Total production of rice in the 1983 to 1986 period exceeded that of 1962 and 1963 by more than four times. Bordering on self-sufficiency in rice, the imports of rice over the same period reflect the pricing policies and subsidies in rice, discussed in Chapter 3. The imports in 1963 and 1964 coincide with lower rice prices at the farm level. Increased prices in 1964 brought production up, once again, to self-sufficiency. Although prices were frozen throughout the 1966–72 period, the subsidies in terms of duty-free fertilizer, research and development, and subsidized agricultural credit kept production increasing to meet demands. When INESPRE moved into the rice trade in 1972, imports kept prices low and production stagnated. The renewed increase in 1979 is perhaps best explained by the influx of credit into the agricultural sector at this time after Hurricane David in 1978.[2] The jump in production in 1983 registered in Table 6.1 would appear to reflect inadequate data. Table 6.2, reporting production of rice paddy, shows no similar jump. As reported in Chapter 3, the terms of trade for the rice sector were falling steadily from 1979 through 1983, improving slightly in 1984 and 1985 before falling again in 1985 (see Table 3.6).

Table 6.1
Production, Importations, and Initial Existence in Warehouses of INESPRE, Apparent Consumption, Population, and Per Capita Consumption of Rice (polished rice, '000 qq, D.R., 1962–86)

	National Production	Imports	Initial Existence	Apparent Consumpt. (1)	Popul. '000	Consumpt. /capita qq
1962	1653.6	0.4		1654.0	3220.6	0.51
1963	1632.9	711.7		2344.6	3315.9	0.71
1964	2035.2	483.8		2519.0	3414.8	0.74
1965	2385.0	1.8		2386.8	3515.3	0.68
1966	2338.6	0.0		2448.6	3619.7	0.68
1967	2504.3	0.4		2504.6	3726.5	0.67
1968	2553.5	386.9		2840.4	3836.9	0.74
1969	2779.3	0.0		2779.3	3950.5	0.70
1970	3827.1	0.1		3827.2	4056.5	0.94
1971	3360.0	0.0		3360.0	4187.9	0.80
1972	3584.0	189.6		3773.6	4311.9	0.88
1973	3916.2	654.5	498.0	4580.7	4431.7	1.03
1974	3460.0	1598.4	488.0	4550.4	4562.3	1.00
1975	3360.0	1091.5	996.0	4660.5	4696.8	0.99
1976	4208.2	703.8	787.0	5011.0	4835.2	1.04
1977	4216.0	1421.4	688.0	5340.4	4977.7	1.07
1978	4698.5	230.9	985.0	4576.4	5124.3	0.89
1979	5456.0		1338.0	6116.0	5299.0	1.15
1980	5723.0	890.1	678.0	6586.4	5458.0	1.21
1981	5707.5	1388.5	704.7	5990.8	5622.0	1.07
1982	5764.3		1810.0	5725.3	5785.0	0.99
1983	7116.9		1849.0	6617.7*	5961.9	1.11
1984	7252.4		2348.2	8115.4*	6101.8	1.33
1985	7065.6	485.0	1385.2	7803.4*	6242.7	1.25
1986	6545.3	2621.0	1132.4	7976.2*	6381.0	1.25

(1) Apparent consumption is calculated on the basis of the sum of production, imports, and initial existence minus final existence.
Final existence 1982—1,849,000 qq.
(*) Calculated.
Source: For 1973–86, CAPA, "Estudio Sobre el Rol del Estado en la Comercialización del Arroz," 1987, pp. 6–21; for 1962–72, Munguía, 1975, p. 219.

Over the same period, the population of the Dominican Republic almost doubled, and per capita consumption of rice more than doubled to over one-third of a pound per person per day (see Table 6.1). As pointed out earlier, the low rice prices had the effect of encouraging rice consumption and steering consumer eating habits away from root crops.

The fourfold increase in rice production over these 25 years was due both to increases in harvested acreage and to increases in productivity, as illustrated in Table 6.2.

Table 6.2
Area Harvested, Production, and Productivity of National Rice Paddy, 1964–86

Year	Production 000 qqs	Area Harvested 000 tareas	Yield qq/tarea
1964	3113.6	940.4	3.3
1965	3647.5	1100.7	3.3
1966	3985.1	1224.5	3.3
1967	3752.1	1182.5	3.2
1968	4063.4	1160.7	3.5
1969	4638.6	1208.4	3.8
1970	4704.8	1319.7	3.6
1971	4748.1	1200.0	4.0
1972	4493.6	1280.0	3.5
1973	4995.2	1364.9	3.7
1974	5810.8	1248.0	4.7
1975	5927.0	1150.0	5.2
1976	6556.5	1460.2	4.5
1977	6899.2	1360.0	5.1
1978	7862.4	1460.0	5.4
1979	8422.4	1600.0	5.3
1980	8906.2	1773.0	5.0
1981	8968.9	1769.0	5.1
1982	10010.5	1642.0	6.1
1983	11212.2	1896.0	5.9
1984	11658.4	1877.7	6.2
1985	11436.0	1753.6	6.5
1986	10069.6	1558.2	6.5

Source: CAPA, 1987, p. 6–2.

Irrigation projects expanded the area available for rice production. The area harvested in 1983 was more than double that of 1964. Improvements in rice varieties, as well as increased use of fertilizers and pesticides, increased yields from about 3.3 qq per *tarea* in 1964 through 1967, to 6.5 qq per *tarea* in 1985 and 1986.

The agrarian reform sector has made a major contribution to rice production in the Dominican Republic and has also experienced similar increases in productivity. Tables 6.3 and 6.4 illustrate the extent of agrarian reform participation in rice production and the increases in productivity that occurred over the 1975 to 1986 period.

In 1975, of the rice area harvested in the country 48.3 percent belonged to the agrarian reform sector, yielding 43 percent of the production of rice. As a share of production and area harvested, this was larger than any year since that time and reflects, to some extent, the early efforts of the IAD to exercise control over production on the rice collectives despite unfavorable prices. Agrarian reform sector production

Table 6.3
Area Harvested, Production, and Productivity of IAD Rice Paddy,
1975–86

Year	Production 000 qqs	Area Harvested 000 tareas	Yield qq/tarea
1975	2550.0	555.2	4.6
1976	2313.0	638.4	3.6
1977	2799.3	624.0	4.5
1978	2770.1	554.0	5.0
1979	3123.3	589.3	5.3
1980	3100.2	673.9	4.6
1981	3680.1	733.1	5.0
1982	3725.1	620.6	6.0
1983	4596.5	744.2	6.2
1984	4016.9	672.2	6.0
1985	3489.5	618.5	5.6
1986	3920.9	619.5	6.3

Sources: IAD annual bulletins; 1975–78 Rodríguez-Núñez, 1985, p. 74, as from
IAD.

Table 6.4
Contribution of IAD Sector to Rice Production in the Dominican
Republic, 1975–86

	as % National Production	as % Harvested Area
1975	43.0%	48.3%
1976	35.3%	43.7%
1977	40.6%	45.9%
1978	35.2%	37.9%
1979	37.1%	36.8%
1980	34.8%	38.0%
1981	41.0%	41.4%
1982	37.2%	37.8%
1983	41.0%	39.3%
1984	34.5%	35.8%
1985	30.5%	35.3%
1986	38.9%	39.8%

Source: Calculated from Tables 6.2 and 6.3.

averaged 37.4 percent of national production over the 1975–86 period
and 40.0 percent of the area harvested.

Although for most years, between 1975 and 1986, agrarian reform
sector productivity lagged behind the national average, Figure 6.1 would
indicate that since 1979, when much of the reorganization of the reform

projects began (in terms of shifting to the associative structure), agrarian reform sector rice productivity has been catching up with the national average. The national average in rice productivity exceeded the IAD average by an average of .6 qq per *tarea* over the 1975 to 1979 period; from 1979 to 1986 that difference dropped to .2 qq per *tarea*. This lends support to the theory that the associative structure yields more efficient production than the individual and collective project structures.

Figure 6.1
Yields: National and IAD
(qq/ta Rice Paddy)

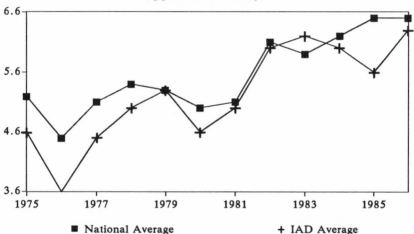

■ National Average   + IAD Average

One reason for the lag between agrarian reform and private sector rice productivity may be a shortage of credit to the reform sector. Private sector rice producers, unlike agrarian reform sector rice producers, may obtain credit for production from the Central Bank and private institutions as well as from the Banco Agrícola.[3] Although availability of data makes it impossible to determine whether in fact credit has been adequate to meet the needs of the private sector, it is clear that credit to the agrarian reform sector in rice has not been adequate.

Table 6.5 shows the total credit disbursed by the Banco Agrícola for agrarian reform sector rice over the 1975 to 1986 period relative to the *tareas* reported harvested. Since no other institution has been approved to extend credit to the agrarian reform sector, this represents the total available formal credit.

Although the amount of available credit per *tarea* has increased steadily, it has not kept pace with the cost of production as estimated by the SEA. Table 6.6 illustrates the difference in cost per *tarea* and credit per *tarea* in absolute terms and as a percentage of cost over the 1979 to 1986 period. The deficit in credit represents an average of 52.7 percent of total cost per *tarea*, although it fluctuates from year to year.

Table 6.5
Financing of IAD Rice Projects, 1975–86

Year	Tareas 000	Amount Disbursed 000 DR$	Credit/Tarea DR$
1975	555.2	6916.0	12.46
1976	638.4	8372.4	13.11
1977	624.0	9970.0	15.98
1978	554.0	10675.0	19.27
1979	589.3	11102.0	18.84
1980	673.9	21757.0	32.29
1981	733.1	18935.8	25.83
1982	620.6	28925.8	46.61
1983	744.2	32473.7	43.63
1984	672.2	38205.2	56.84
1985	618.5	59895.6	96.84
1986	619.5	46543.1	75.13
	(1)	(2)	(3)

Sources: (1) Table 6.3.
(2) IAD Boletín Informativo Anual, 1986; Delgado, 1983, p. 195.
(3) Calculated.

Table 6.6
Cost of Production Relative to Financing Provided, 1979–86 (DR$)

	BAGRICOLA Credit /Tarea	Estimated Cost /Tarea	Credit Deficit	Deficit as % of Cost/Tarea
1979	18.84	48.74	29.90	61.3%
1980	32.29	60.81	28.52	46.9%
1981	25.83	72.82	46.99	64.5%
1982	46.61	73.20	26.59	36.3%
1983	43.63	88.67	45.04	50.8%
1984	56.84	129.41	72.57	56.1%
1985	96.84	175.81	78.97	44.9%
1986	75.13	192.42	117.29	61.0%
	(1)	(2)	(3)	(3)

Sources: (1) Table 6.5.
(2) CAPA, 1987, p. 6–42.
(3) Calculated.

The calculation of cost of production per *tarea* shown in Table 6.7, includes labor cost that may or may not be provided by the beneficiary himself. Even so, the labor cost represents less than 40 percent of the total costs. Thus, given the nature of agricultural production and the very tight cash flow of the average beneficiary, it is clear that adequate credit has not been available for reform sector rice. Further, the personnel of the IAD point out that much of the credit destined for production among

Table 6.7
Cost of Production per Tarea, 1986

		Quantity		Cost DR$
Preparation	Seedbed			6.99
	Land			48.00
Prod Inputs	Fertilizer	0.9168	qq	17.42
	Seeds	0.1755	qq	10.53
	Insecticide	0.0742	lt	2.19
	Fungicides	0.3409	lb	1.96
	Herbicides	0.0222	lb	2.24
Labor Inputs	Sowing	1	(D/H)	12.00
	Weeding	1	(D/H)	10.00
	Application	2.3	(D/H)	27.58
	Harvest	1.875	(D/H)	22.50
Interest on use of Capital		6	mths	14.27
Other		0.54	(D/H)	6.47
Internal Transportation				
Payment to INDRHI				
Clean Canals				
Packing of Products				
Total Cost per Tarea				182.15

Source: SEA, *Plan Operativa, 1987.*

the reform beneficiaries is diverted to consumption, so that the remainder is insufficient to finance agricultural inputs at the recommended levels. They emphasize that this is the major reason for lower productivity in the reform sector rice.

It would be desireable to determine whether real profits have improved for the agrarian reform beneficiaries as the reform projects have switched to the associative structure. Although local leaders have reported that profits indeed increased, we are unable to show this empirically on a national level.

Tables 6.8 and 6.9 show net benefits per *tarea* and real net benefits per *tarea*, respectively, for reform sector rice. Unfortunately, these figures are not particularly indicative of the real profits the beneficiaries have earned. In the first place, production may not always be reported. A sizable portion may be consumed in the household or sold through unreported channels.[4] And, equally important, neither estimated cost per *tarea* nor credit disbursed by the Agricultural Bank per *tarea* is an adequate proxy of the actual costs of production per *tarea*.

Beneficiaries certainly do not follow the optimal production plan as outlined by the SEA. They may decide, for example, not to replant a second crop but to cut costs by harvesting a second crop, or *retoño*,

Table 6.8
Net Benefit per Tarea to IAD Sector, 1975–86
(net cost and net credit)

	Yield qqs/ tarea	Inespre Price /qq	$ Value /Tarea	Net Benefit/Tarea Net Cost	Net Credit
1975	4.6	10.02	46.00		33.54
1976	3.6	10.02	36.29		23.17
1977	4.5	10.02	44.93		28.95
1978	5.0	10.02	50.08		30.81
1979	5.3	10.02	53.08	4.34	34.24
1980	4.6	11.53	53.04	−7.77	20.75
1981	5.0	12.41	62.28	−10.54	36.45
1982	6.0	12.41	74.47	1.27	27.86
1983	6.2	12.41	76.62	−12.05	32.99
1984	6.0	19.12	114.29	−15.12	57.45
1985	5.6	29.25	165.02	−10.79	68.18
1986	6.3	27.78	175.85	−16.57	100.72
	(1)	(2)	(3)	(4)	(4)

Sources: (1) Table 6.2.
      (2) Calculated from Table 3.6.
      (3) Calculated.
      (4) Calculated with Table 6.6.

Table 6.9
Real Net Benefit per Tarea to IAD Sector, 1975–86
(net cost and net credit)

	CPI	Real Net Benefit /Tarea Net Cost	Net Credit
1975	100.0		33.54
1976	107.9		21.48
1977	121.7		23.79
1978	130.3		23.64
1979	142.3	3.05	24.06
1980	166.1	−4.68	12.50
1981	178.6	−5.90	20.41
1982	192.4	0.66	14.48
1983	205.7	−5.86	16.04
1984	256.0	−5.91	22.44
1985	352.1	−3.06	19.36
1986	386.4	−4.29	26.07
	(1)	(2)	(2)

Sources: (1) Calculated from Banco Central, *Boletín Mensual*, January 1987; and Rodríguez-Núñez, 1985, p. 78.
      (2) Calculated with Table 6.8.

from the first planting. Additionally, as already explained, beneficiaries may or may not spend all the credit they receive from the Agricultural Bank on production, and it is impossible to determine if they have made expenditures out of savings or local credit sources. To a certain extent, however, at the end of harvest the beneficiary's profit is that which is left to him after paying his debt to the Banco Agrícola.

When net benefits are adjusted by the consumer price index in Table 6.9, it can be seen that although they vary significantly from year to year, there is no indication of either improvement or deterioration over the period of reorganization of the reform projects.

At the Local Level

Improvements in production per hectare, after reorganization to the associative structure from both the individual and the collective project structures, are much more clearly defined for the particular cases.

Figure 6.2 gives an indication of the improvement in yield for the individual beneficiaries who formed associatives. The productivity yields of the "Asentamiento Campesino No. 14" (AC–14) Camú, which contains the association Sergio A. Cabrera, jump from an average of 2.5 qq per *tarea* over the 1975 to 1979 period, before Sergio A. Cabrera reorganized as an associative, to an average of 6.7 qq per *tarea* from 1980 to 1986. Likewise, the yields of AC–18 Rincón, to which Padre Fantino pertains, improve from 4.3 qq per *tarea*, before the members of Padre Fantino associated in 1980, to 7.0 qq per *tarea* after that point.[5] Although national productivity was increasing over the 1975–86 period, both of these settlements began with yields below the national average and experienced yields well above the national average after their reorganization to associatives. Similar increases in productivity occurred in the rice zones Mao-Valverde and Rincón after the breakdown of the collectives into associatives in 1983. Vásquez Quintero, Bermúdez, and Santa Clara, which have been discussed as case studies, are among these associatives; but in fact the majority of the other collectives in the area underwent a comparable transformation between 1983 and the passage of the associative law in 1985.

Figure 6.3 demonstrates the high productivity yields experienced in the rice zones Mao-Valverde and Rincón, with the reorganization from collectives to associatives, over the 1983 to 1985 period. Certainly it is very early to evaluate a transformation that occurred so recently, but the numbers would indicate, at least, that the effects have not been negative.

Further evidence of the experience of the collective farms is found in the distribution of profits per beneficiary for the ex-collective farm Vásquez Quintero, which reorganized into an associative in 1983. When profits are adjusted by the consumer price index, it can be seen that

**Figure 6.2
Yields: Ex-Individual Projects
(qq/ta Rice Paddy)**

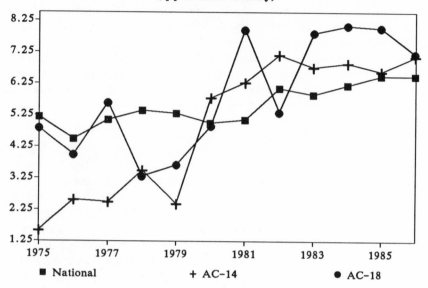

■ National   + AC-14   ● AC-18

**Figure 6.3
Yields: Ex-Collective Projects
(qq/ta Rice Paddy)**

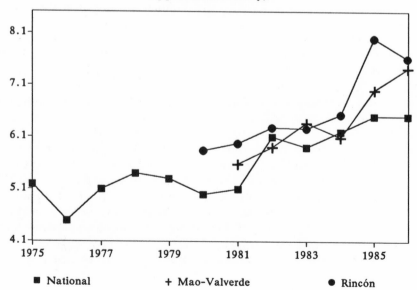

■ National   + Mao-Valverde   ● Rincón

although real profits were initially high, by 1980 they had fallen substantially, increasing again after the breakdown of the collective into an associative in January of 1983 (see Table 6.10). This parallels the beneficiary reports of initial enthusiasm for the work, later discouragement and suspicion of others' labor input, and renewed incentive with the parcellation of the collective farm. As explained earlier in the chapter, however, "profit," which is actually the difference between the sale value of rice that the collective or associative handles and the credit to the beneficiary from the Banco Agrícola, is an imperfect measure of productive efficiency.

Table 6.10
Distribution of Profits per Beneficiary for Vásquez Quintero, 1974-86

	Profit/ Beneficiary	CPI	Real Profit/ Beneficiary
1974	1994.84	100.0	1994.84
1975	2237.94	114.5	1954.53
1976	1239.19	123.5	1003.39
1977	1023.04	139.3	734.41
1978	824.52*	149.2	552.63*
1979	2289.87	162.9	1405.69
1980	1509.57	190.2	793.68
1981	-215.97	204.5	-105.61
1982	428.26	220.3	194.40
1983	1111.47*	235.6	471.76*
1984	2676.82	293.1	913.28
1985	4918.75	403.2	1219.93
1986	2334.85*	442.2	528.01*
	(1)	(2)	(3)

*First harvest only.
Sources: (1) For 1974-83, Gutiérrez, 1983b; for 1984-86, IAD, Rincón.
(2) Table 6.9.
(3) Calculated.

Finally, the exposure to risk of the agrarian reform beneficiaries is demonstrated in the farm records of Sergio A. Cabrera. For the spring 1986 rice crop the net income of the 60 people who participated in the credit program ranged from a loss of DR$4740.65 to a profit of DR$10,898.53, with mean net income at DR$1920.79. The standard deviation of net income was DR$3964.08, yielding a coefficient of variation of over 200 percent. (See Appendix Table A.7 and Figure 6.4.) It is clear, however, as pointed out by Carter (1987), that accounting practices vary across individuals. Other beneficiaries may have had other sources of investment capital in addition to the credit payment. Certainly these records may overstate the exposure to risk; nevertheless, risk exposure is quite significant, and the value of the associative in providing group credit to cover losses and ensure continued credit is clear.

Figure 6.4
Profits: Sergio A. Cabrera first season, 1986

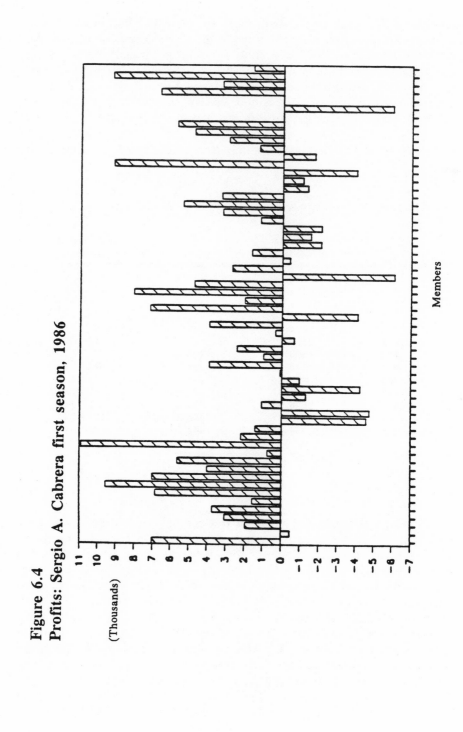

(Thousands)

Members

Empirical evidence exists, therefore, to support our conclusions in Chapter 5: that an associative structure can yield more efficient production by relieving the risk burden on the beneficiaries while still providing full incentive for effort.

ASSOCIATIONS OF FARMERS MAKING THEMSELVES HEARD

Currently in the Dominican Republic land reform has been taken off the back burner. Joaquín Balaguer, in a speech to farmers in Yamasá, in mid-July, made the following declaration:

> Agrarian reform, . . . is the bride of the current government. It is the most important social work that there is to carry out in the Dominican Republic. For that reason, it is to that work that I have dedicated the last days of my life. It is the only work over which, if I realize it, I will descend peacefully to the tomb.[6] (*Listín Diario*, July 12, 1987)

In the same speech he continued to warn the rural workers against spontaneously invading the land, asking them, rather to be patient for the government to designate the adequate lands for the purpose. He concluded with a promise for continued dialogue with the rural poor saying, "I hope that in that dialogue we speak one to one, with absolute frankness. That you tell me what you want, you tell me your necessities, and that I also tell you with the same frankness what are the possibilities of the government."[7] This speech is only one of a great many of late, as Balaguer makes weekly weekend excursions to the *campo* to dedicate irrigation projects and new land reform settlements, and for continued dialogue with the *campesinos*.

Needless to say, the rural poor community has responded positively to Balaguer's words, although perhaps they have less faith that his words will be carried out by his administration. Land invasions are frequent, as are gatherings of rural poor, at the local IAD offices as well as in the capital, to demand land.

Associations of farmers have formed federations of representatives on a regional level, as for example the federation Padre Cavero in the Rincón area. Also on a national level, a general committee to represent all agrarian reform beneficiaries was formed in 1982 with 36 members. The members have worked to fight against the power of the IAD to cancel the rights of a beneficiary to his plot of land and to obtain definitive titles to the land; they have also participated in seminars at the national level dealing with the administration of reform projects.

Luis Castro spoke optimistically of this relatively new power of the farmers to make themselves heard, saying that in earlier years the IAD administrators represented the beneficiaries to the government, but that now they represent themselves and that consequently they are much more able to communicate their true situation.

After 25 years of experience of land reform in the Dominican Republic, many lessons have been learned as to how such a thing should be carried out. But agrarian reform agency personnel come and go, and continuity in policy is easily lost. Lessons learned in past administrations must be relearned with the new personnel. Unquestionably, those who have learned the most are those who have been most intimately involved, the beneficiaries themselves. From that point of view it is encouraging that they are finally in a position to share that education among themselves and make themselves heard on a national level.

CONCLUSION

The experience in the Dominican Republic, with the transformation within the agrarian reform rice sector from both the collective and individual project structures to an intermediate associative structure, provides evidence that if properly administrated, an associative can provide scale benefits without destroying individual initiative.

The local leaders, who have fought for many years for the adoption of the associative structure, believe unequivocably that it provides the best of both worlds: all the benefits to collective action provided by the collectives and the freedom and incentive for individual initiative provided by the individual project structure. The empirical evidence, on the productivity of agrarian reform sector rice relative to national rice productivity, shows that since the reorganization of the projects began, productivity in the reform sector has been catching up with the national average. At the local level, the evidence is more dramatic, with large increases in productivity after the projects reorganized into associatives. Perhaps most encouraging is the fact that the associative structure has allowed for the development of strong and responsible leadership among the reform beneficiaries, such that they are now in a position to make their needs known to the relevant government agencies and to function independently with the private sector.

Thus, the evidence substantiates the theoretical implications of Chapter 5: that the associative structure pareto dominates the individual structure by removing the risk burden from risk-averse beneficiaries and by capitalizing on the economies of scale inherent in the provision of administrator effort, effort of key importance in the production function of reform sector rice. Likewise, the associative structure of organization pareto dominates the collective, where profits are divided equally among all, by returning to the beneficiary the full marginal benefit of his effort. Finally, as shown in training in administration, they may efficiently "hire" their own administrator and independently seek an institution willing to absorb the risk inherent in agricultural production.

Certainly the theoretical study here has focused rather narrowly on the key role of the administrator in providing effort toward production and on the problems of incentives and risk sharing among the agents involved. These elements, however, were drawn from specific case studies of agrarian reform projects in the Dominican Republic and were shown to be the essential questions of project organization. With this focus, contributions have been made to aspects of organization theory not yet fully explored in the relevant literature. Ample issues for further research have been uncovered, including a more careful treatment of credit contracts, relationships between supporting government agency personnel, and such problems as the optimal size of an agrarian reform project, to name only a few.

The experience of land reform in the Dominican Republic in many ways typifies the experience of Latin America. It should be remembered, however, that the theoretical analysis was made only after a very careful examination of the institutional framework in the Dominican Republic, the specific factors affecting rice production, and the organizational problems of particular rice projects in the country. The assumptions made as the basis of the analysis certainly may not be appropriate for other countries.

Nevertheless, many of the countries in Latin America have experienced similar struggles in their attempt to find an appropriate structure for the reform projects. Certainly the appropriate structure must be specific to the crops grown as well as to the institutions in the country. However, the issues of administration, credit for insurance as well as for production, and worker incentive have been shown to be critical all over Latin America. Thus, the relevance of this study, with regard to the questions it approaches, is indeed widespread.

NOTES

1. This should not be taken as a viewpoint entirely representative of all beneficiaries. To a certain extent, the leaders have participated more extensively in the activities of the reform projects and have devoted more study to the problems they encounter and are, therefore, very good sources of information and judgments. But by the same token, since they have invested a sizable portion of their lives in fighting for the associative structure, they have all the more reason to speak favorably of it.

2. See Table 3.3.

3. Table A.2 in the Appendix shows the credit per *tarea* from the Banco Agrícola to the rice sector. As shown in Table A.3, an increasingly larger proportion of credit for rice from the Banco Agrícola over the 1975–84 period was destined to the agrarian reform sector, as the Central Bank and private institutions played an increasingly larger role in private sector rice production. Table 3.3 shows the relative shares in total agricultural production credit of the Banco Agrícola, the Central Bank, and private institutions.

4. With prices kept low for rice in the Dominican Republic, significant quantities have been smuggled to Haiti, where prices may be considerably higher.

5. It is not clear what changes may be occurring on other farms of the same settlements. AC–18 includes 297 beneficiaries, of which 59 pertain to the association Padre Fantino. AC–14 includes 308 beneficiaries, of which 59 pertain to the association Sergio A. Cabrera. (See Table A.4 in the Appendix.) It is also not clear whether all the farms of the settlements were reporting their yields. Table A.5 in the Appendix reveals the *tareas* reported harvested, while Table A.4 notes the total *tareas* in the farms in question.

6. "La Reforma Agraria, . . . es la novia del Gobierno actual. Es la obra social más importante que hay que llevar a cabo en la República Dominicana. Por eso, a esa obra he consagrado los últimos dias de mi vida. Es la única obra la cual, si la realizo bajaría tranquilo a la tumba."

7. "espero que en ese diálogo nos hablemos de tú a tú, con absoluta franqueza. Que ustedes me digan lo que quieren, me indiquen sus necesidades y que yo también les diga con la misma franqueza cuáles son las posibilidades del Gobierno."

Appendix

Proof of Proposition 2

Restating the first–best problem, one has

(A) $\underset{e_1,e_2,\phi_1,\phi_2}{\text{Max}} E[m \cdot nx \,(e_1,e_2) + \sum_{i=1}^{m \cdot n} \theta_i - m \cdot n\phi_1 - m\phi_2]$, s.t.

(A.1) $\quad U_1(\phi_1) - V_1(e_1) = W_1^\circ$

(A.2) $\quad U_2(\phi_2) - V_2(e_2) = W_2^\circ$

with first–order conditions

(A.3) $\quad U_1'(\phi_1)x_1(e_1,e_2) = V_1'(e_1)$

(A.4) $\quad U_2'(\phi_2)x_2(e_1,e_2) = V_2'(e_2)/n$

yielding solution $e_1^*, e_2^*, \phi_1^*, \phi_2^*$.

In the hierarchical rent contract with the specified credit mechanism the government agency's problem is the following:

(B) $\underset{e_1,e_2,Q_1,Q_2}{\text{Max}} E(mQ_2 + \sum_{i=1}^{m \cdot n} \theta_i)$ s.t

(B.1) $U_1(x(e_1,e_2) + \theta - (Q_1 + \theta)) - V_1(e_1) = W_1^{\circ}$

(B.2) $U_2(nQ_1 - Q_2) - V_2(e_2)) = W_2^{\circ}$

Taking first–order conditions,

(B.3) $U_1'(x(e_1,e_2) - Q_1)x_1(e_1,e_2) = V_1'(e_1)$

(B.4) $U_2'(nQ_1 - Q_2)x_2(e_1,e_2) = V_2'(e_2)/n$

Solving (B.1) – (B.4) yields the solution $e_1{}^q, e_2{}^q, Q_1{}^q, Q_2{}^q$, where $e_1{}^q = e_1{}^*$, $e_2{}^q = e_2{}^*$, $Q_1{}^q = x(e_1{}^*,e_2{}^*) - \phi_1{}^*$ and $Q_2{}^q = nx(e_1{}^*,e_2{}^*) - n\phi_1{}^* - \phi_2{}^*$.

Again, this cannot be stated without proof, but it is shown by the same argument as in the two–person case; namely, $e_1{}^*, e_2{}^*, \phi_1{}^*, \phi_2{}^*$ satisfy problem (A) so that $e_1{}^q, e_2{}^q, Q_1{}^q, Q_2{}^q$, so defined, satisfy the conditions for (B). Since the solutions to (A) and (B) are unique, it must be the case that $e_1{}^q, e_2{}^q, Q_1{}^q, Q_2{}^q$, as defined, provide the unique solution to (B).

To see how the administrator reacts to the agency's choice of $Q_2{}^q$, one must look at his problem:

(C) Max $U_2(nQ_1 - Q_2{}^q) - V_2(e_2)$ s.t.
     e_1, e_2, Q_1

(C.1) $U_1(x(e_1,e_2) + \theta - (Q_1 + \theta)) - V_1(e_1) = W_1^{\circ}$

Taking first-order conditions and rewriting, the following result:

(C.2) $U_1'(x(e_1,e_2) - Q_1)x_1(e_1,e_2) = V_1'(e_1)$

(C.3) $U_2'(nQ_1 - Q_2)x_2(e_1,e_2) = V_2'(e_2)/n$

These, with (C.1), coincide with the first–order conditions of the government agency in (B); so that given $Q_2{}^q$, the administrator will choose $e_1{}^q, e_2{}^q, Q_1{}^q$.

Finally, there is the beneficiary's problem:

(D) Max $U_1(x(e_1,e_2{}^q) + \theta - (Q_1{}^q + \theta)) - V_1(e_1)$
     e_1

which yields his first–order condition:

(D.1) $U_1'(x(e_1,e_2{}^q) - Q_1{}^q)x_1(e_1,e_2{}^q) = V_1'(e_1)$

Since his first-order condition coincides with that of the government agency and the administrator, given $e_2{}^q, Q_1{}^q$, his choice of e_1 must be $e_1{}^q$; consequently, both income and effort levels for all parties will be the same as in the first-best case.

Proof of Proposition 3

As in the hierarchical rent contract with the specified credit mechanism, the government agency's problem is as follows:

(E) $\displaystyle\operatorname*{Max}_{e_1, e_2, Q_1, Q_2} E\left(mQ_2 + \sum_{i=1}^{m \cdot n} \theta_i\right)$ s.t

(E.1) $U_1[(1/n)(nx(e_1, e_2) - Q_1)] - V_1(e_1) = W_1{}^\circ$

(E.²) $U_2(Q_1 - Q_2) - V_2(e_2) = W_2{}^\circ$

Taking partial derivatives with respect to the choice variables yields first-order conditions that may be combined to get the following:

(E.3) $U_1'(x(e_1, e_2) - 1/n \cdot Q_1) x_1(e_1, e_2) = V_1'(e_1)$

(E.4) $U_2'(Q_1 - Q_2) x_2(e_1, e_2) = V_2'(e_2)/n$

Solving (E.1) – (E.4) yields the solution $e_1{}^c, e_2{}^c, Q_1{}^c, Q_2{}^c$, where $e_1{}^c = e_1{}^*$, $e_2{}^c = e_2{}^*$, $Q_1{}^c = n[x(e_1{}^*, e_2{}^*) - \phi_1{}^*] = nQ_1{}^q$, and $Q_2{}^c = nx(e_1{}^*, e_2{}^*) - n\phi_1{}^* - \phi_2{}^* = Q_2{}^q$. By the same argument as in Proposition 2, $e_1{}^*, e_2{}^*, \phi_1{}^*, \phi_2{}^*$ satisfy problem (A) so that $e_1{}^c, e_2{}^c, Q_1{}^c, Q_2{}^c$, so defined, satisfy the conditions for (E). Since the solutions to (A) and (E) are unique, it must be the case that $e_1{}^c, e_2{}^c, Q_1{}^c, Q_2{}^c$, as defined, provide the unique solution to (E).

To see how the administrator reacts to the agency's choice of $Q_2{}^q$, consider his problem:

(F) $\displaystyle\operatorname*{Max}_{e_1, e_2, Q_1} U_2(Q_1 - Q_2{}^c) - V_2(e_2)$ s.t.

(F.1) $U_1[(1/n)(nx(e_1, e_2) - Q_1)] - V_1(e_1) = W_1{}^\circ$

Taking first-order conditions and rewriting, the following result:

(F.2) $U_1'(x(e_1, e_2) - (1/n)Q_1) x_1(e_1, e_2) = V_1'(e_1)$

(F.3) $U_2'(Q_1 - Q_2{}^c)x_2(e_1,e_2) = V_2'(e_2)/n$

These, with (F.1), coincide with those of the government agency in (E), so that given $Q_2{}^c$, the administrator will choose $e_1{}^c, e_2{}^c$, $Q_1{}^c$.

Thus, the agency could choose a quota such that the administrator provides first–best effort. The administrator, likewise, would choose a quota, $Q_1{}^c$, for the group of beneficiaries such that if each provides optimal effort, each will be just able to remain at his minimum utility and pay the quota.

However, since the administrator cannot enforce effort on the part of the beneficiaries, their problem must be considered:

$$\underset{e_{1i}}{\text{Max }} U_{1i}\left[(1/n)(x(e_{1i},e_2{}^c) + \sum_{j\neq i}^{n} x(e_{1j},e_2{}^c) - Q_1{}^c)\right] - V_{1i}(e_{1i})$$

for all $i = 1, 2, \ldots, n$ beneficiaries. This yields first order–conditions for all n beneficiaries:

$$(1/n)U_{1i}'\left[(1/n)(x(e_{1i},e_2{}^c) + \sum_{j\neq i}^{n} x(e_{1j},e_2{}^c) - Q_1{}^c)\right]x_1(e_{1i},e_2{}^c) =$$
$$V_{1i}'(e_{1i})$$

where the choice of e_{1i} depends on the beneficiary's conjecture about the others' choices of e_{1j}. In a Cournot-Nash equilibrium, this conjecture must be consistent with what is actually observed; and since all beneficiaries are identical, all must choose the same effort level in equilibrium: $e_{1i} = e_1{}^N$ for all i. Consequently, in equilibrium:

$$(1/n)U_1'\left[(1/n)(nx(e_1{}^N,e_2{}^c) - Q_1{}^c)\right]x_1(e_1{}^N,e_2{}^c) = V_1'(e_1{}^N)$$

We know that $U_1'(\cdot)x_1(\cdot)$ is strictly decreasing in e_1 and $V_1'(\cdot)$ is strictly increasing in e_1. From (E.3),

$$U_1'[x(e_1,e_2{}^c) - (1/n)Q_1{}^c]x_1(e_1,e_2{}^c) = V_1'(e_1)$$

is satisfied at $e_1{}^*$. Therefore,

$$1/n \cdot U_1'[x(e_1,e_2{}^c) - (1/n)Q_1{}^c]x_1(e_1,e_2{}^c) = V_1'(e_1)$$

is satisfied at $e_1{}^N < e_1{}^*$. (See Figure 5.1.)

Table A.1
Financing of the IAD Sector, 1975–86

Year	Amount Disbursed 000 DR$ For Rice	Total	Rice as % of Total
1975	6916.0	7616.0	90.8%
1976	8372.4	9110.2	91.9%
1977	9970.0	11766.3	84.7%
1978	10675.0	12877.6	82.9%
1979	11102.0	12301.9	90.2%
1980	21757.0	25587.5	85.0%
1981	18935.8	22763.2	83.2%
1982	28925.8	35008.2	82.6%
1983	32473.7	39246.2	82.7%
1984	38205.2	44779.5	85.3%
1985	59895.6	75644.4	79.2%
1986	46543.1	54886.0	84.8%
	(1)	(2)	(3)

Sources: (1) *IAD Boletín Informativo Anual, 1986*; Delgado, 1983, p. 195.
(2) IAD, loose sheets, 1987.
(3) Calculated.

Table A.2
Financing of National Rice Projects, 1975–85

Year	Tareas 000	Amount Disbursed 000 DR$	Credit/tarea DR$
1975	1150.0	34700.0	30.17
1976	1460.2	37200.0	25.48
1977	1360.0	32200.0	23.68
1978	1460.0	45500.0	31.16
1979	1600.0	48700.0	30.44
1980	1773.0	59400.0	33.50
1981	1769.0	48574.3	27.46
1982	1642.0	48729.2	29.68
1983	1896.0	51033.4	26.92
1984	1877.7	66949.8	35.66
	(1)	(2)	(3)

Sources: (1) Table 6.3.
(2) For 1981–84, BAGRICOLA, 1985, pp. 154–57;
For 1975–80, Delgado, 1983, p. 195–A.
(3) Calculated.

Table A.3
Financing of IAD Rice Projects as Percentage of Total Financing for Rice by the Banco Agrícola

1975	19.9%
1976	22.5%
1977	31.0%
1978	23.5%
1979	22.8%
1980	36.6%
1981	39.0%
1982	59.4%
1983	63.6%
1984	57.1%

Source: Calculated from Tables A.1 and A.2.

Table A.4
The Cases Studied

Name of Association	Founded	Number of Bene-ficiaries	Ha.	Switched to Assoc.	Mem-bers	Location
Individual->Associative						
Padre Fantino	1963	84	362	1980	59	AC–18 Rincón w/ 297 benfs
Sergio A. Cabrera	1964	78	294··	1980	59	AC–14 Camú w/ 308 benfs
El Esfuerzo	1968	43		1978	59	AC–25 Jaibón-Laguna Salada w/ 541 benfs
Collective->Associative						
Vásquez Quintero	Dec'73	63	199	Jan'83	63	Zona Arrocera Rincón w/ 623 benfs
Bermúdez A, B	1974	88	257	1984	88	Zona Arrocera Mao-Valverde
Divided	late '82					w/ 460 benfs
Santa Clara	1983			1983	88	Zona Arrocera Rincón
Carlos Castillo I,II	1973	40	123			
Divided I & II	1975	20/farm				
Reynaldo Bisono	1973	48	132			

Sources: Carter and Kanel, 1985; Genao and Torres, 1987; Gutiérrez, 1983a and 1983b; Stanfield et al. 1983 and 1986; Stringer, 1986; interviews with author, July 1987.

Table A.5
Tareas Harvested, Production, and Yield per Tarea for AC-18 Rincón and AC-14 Camú, 1975-86

	AC-18 Rincón Tareas Harvested	Production qq	Yield/ tarea	AC-14 Camú Tareas Harvested	Production qq	Yield/ tarea
1975	4527	21910	4.84	4612	7363	1.60
1976	8711	34882	4.00	9354	24007	2.57
1977	5523	31252	5.66	5240	13100	2.50
1978	960	3174	3.31	597	2090	3.50
1979	6158	22579	3.67	6150	15073	2.45
1980	8002	39112	4.89	10201	59073	5.79
1981	7233	57763	7.99	15969	100365	6.28
1982	7368	39536	5.37	12300	88116	7.16
1983	8453	66323	7.85	16291	110209	6.77
1984	17508	141499	8.08	12352	85239	6.90
1985	7560	60580	8.01	7274	48317	6.64
1986	2487	17917	7.20	10495	74607	7.11

Source: IAD, annual bulletins.

Table A.6
Tareas Harvested, Production, and Yield per Tarea for Rice Zones Rincón and Mao-Valverde, 1980-86

	Rincón Tareas Harvested	Production qq	Yield/ tarea	Mao-Valverde Tareas Harvested	Production qq	Yield/ tarea
1980	42295	246868	5.84			
1981	61820	368926	5.97	38728	216039	5.58
1982	61658	386922	6.28	37274	219779	5.90
1983	60000	375809	6.26	30638	195164	6.37
1984	34738	226789	6.53	35634	217064	6.09
1985	14681	117448	8.00	29576	207032	7.00
1986	19420	147808	7.61	32363	240211	7.42

Source: IAD, annual bulletins.

Table A.7
Costs, Value of Production, and Profit for Each Member: Sergio A. Cabrera First Season, 1986

Member	Costs	Value of Production	Profit
1 Ramón Reynosa	11037.95	18060.12	7022.17
2 José Toribio	15523.31	15053.22	-470.09
3 Mireya González	13420.34	15348.84	1928.50
4 Gabriel Trinidad	15530.81	18581.16	3050.35
5 Francisco Fuentes	14875.56	18587.40	3711.84
6 Bautizta González	7637.25	9197.76	1560.51
7 Mario Vásquez	9914.33	16753.62	6839.29
8 Antolín Pérez	9528.58	19088.92	9560.34
9 Carlixta Malena	12155.81	19191.90	7036.09
10 Francisco Siri	13674.71	17667.78	3993.07
11 Juan Mejía	14321.06	19964.10	5643.04
12 Aurelio Mercedes	14131.74	14873.82	742.08
13 Tomás de la Cruz	7883.09	18781.62	10898.53
14 Bienvenido Monegro	15903.27	18097.56	2194.29
15 Antonio Acosta	13477.12	14881.62	1404.50
16 Juan Polanco	14440.10	9866.22	-4573.88
17 Elso Germosen	17120.81	12380.16	-4740.65
18 Augustín González	15035.39	16102.32	1066.93
19 Altagracia Coronado	16596.11	15306.72	-1289.39
20 Eduardo Corniella	15666.53	11437.14	-4229.39
21 Silverio Rosario	15093.12	14137.50	-955.62
22 Felix Trinidad	14051.21	14133.60	82.39
23 José Díaz	13877.08	17785.56	3908.48
24 Luis Antonio Castro	16468.55	17433.00	964.45
25 Pedro Ventura	16756.93	19188.00	2431.07
26 Arcenio Veras	13017.36	12359.10	-658.26
27 Francisco González	13984.64	14330.94	346.30
28 María Ramírez	14593.59	18513.30	3919.71
29 Luciano Polanco	16230.49	12164.88	-4065.61
30 Pedro Santos	12514.43	19694.22	7179.79
31 Juana Ortega	13739.97	15759.90	2019.93
32 Cesareo Gómez	11928.61	19986.72	8058.11
33 José Antonio Madera	14230.99	18974.28	4743.29
34 Juliano González	13979.90	7892.04	-6087.86
35 Ana Justicia Siri	9665.35	12383.28	2717.93
36 Luis Sánchez	11083.35	10696.14	-387.21
37 Rosalio González	10776.35	12418.38	1642.03
38 Saturnino Jiménez	13831.07	11763.18	-2067.89
39 Juan Guzmán	8933.92	7428.72	-1505.20
40 Juana Cordero	11602.45	9501.96	-2100.49
41 Nicholas Martínez	10970.02	12157.08	1187.06
42 Eugenio Medina	11464.24	14699.10	3234.86
43 Ciriaco Fantigua	13329.69	18727.02	5397.33
44 Wencelao Florentino	10686.46	13975.26	3288.80
45 José Santos	8646.22	7313.28	-1332.94

Table A.7 (Continued)
Costs, Value of Production, and Profit for Each Member: Sergio A. Cabrera First Season, 1986

Member	Costs	Value of Production	Profit
46 Aurelio Morillo	11862.07	10785.06	-1077.01
47 Jesús María Sosa	14301.29	10299.12	-4002.17
48 Cerrado Congirón	13405.83	22580.22	9174.39
49 Antonio González	12850.25	11142.95	-1707.30
50 Francisco Irrizarri	8137.75	9423.18	1285.43
51 Juan Antonio Reyes	16705.02	19608.42	2903.40
52 Ovidir Chávez	11089.62	15858.18	4768.56
53 Ramón Rodríguez	8433.46	14163.90	5730.44
54 Antonio Irrizarri	6837.01	6837.01	0.00
55 Andres Peralta	20261.56	14292.72	-5968.84
56 Cirilo Antonio Tejada	11288.54	11288.54	0.00
57 José Galvez	8748.33	15425.28	6676.95
58 Manuel Malena	15587.45	18866.64	3279.19
59 Rafael Coronado	6599.07	15867.54	9268.47
60 Ramón Tavárez	14081.74	15688.92	1607.18
Total	769518.84	884766.12	115247.27
Mean	12825.31	14746.10	1920.79
Std Dev	2878.82	3775.09	3964.08
Coef of Variation	0.22	0.26	2.06

Source: Records from the Association Sergio A. Cabrera.

References

Adams, Dale W. "Effects of Finance on Rural Development." In *Undermining Rural Development with Cheap Credit*. Edited by D. Adams, D. Graham, and J. Von Pischke. Boulder: Westview Press, 1984.

Adams, Dale W., D. Graham, and J. D. Von Pischke, eds. *Undermining Rural Development with Cheap Credit*. Boulder, Colo.: Westview Press, 1984.

Adams, Dale W., and Jerry Ladman. "Rural Poor and the Recent Performance of Formal Rural Financial Markets in the Dominican Republic." *Canadian Journal of Agricultural Economics* 26:1 (1978).

Adams, Dale W., and Norman Rask. "Economics of Cost-Share Leases in Less-developed Countries." *American Journal of Agricultural Economics* 50 (November 1968): 935-42.

Adams, Dale W., and A. A. Pablo Romero. "Group Lending to the Rural Poor in the Dominican Republic: A Stunted Innovation." *Canadian Journal of Agricultural Economics* 29 (July 1981): 217-24.

Alberts, Tom. *Agrarian Reform and Rural Poverty: A Case Study of Peru*. Boulder, Colo.: Westview Press, 1983.

Aquino González, Carlos. *Fundamentos Para una Estrategia de Desarrollo Agrícola*. Santiago: Centro de Investigaciones Económicas y Alimenticias, Instituto Superior de Agricultura, 1978.

Arrow, Kenneth J. "Informational Structure of the Firm." *American Economic Review* 75:2 (May 1985): 303-307.

Augelli, John P. "Agricultural Colonization in the Dominican Republic." *Economic Geography* 38:1 (January 1962): 15-27.

Baker, Chester B. "Role of Credit in the Economic Development of Small Farmer Agriculture." *AID Spring Review of Small Farmer Credit*, Vol. XIX, June 1973, No. SR119: 43-70.

Bardhan, P. K. "Interlocking Factor Markets and Agrarian Development: A Review of Issues." *Oxford Economic Papers* 32 (1980): 82-98.

Bardhan, P. K. and T. N. Srinivasan. "Cropsharing and Tenancy in Agriculture: A Theoretical and Empirical Analysis." *American Economic Review* 61 (March 1971): 48-64.

Barraclough, Solon. "Agrarian Reform and Structural Change in Latin America: The Chilean Case." *Journal of Development Studies* 8:2 (January 1972): 163-81.

_____. *Agrarian Structure in Latin America*. Lexington, Mass.: Lexington Books, 1973.

_____. "Agricultural Finance and Rural Credit in Poor Countries: Comment." *World Development* 4:2 (July 1976): 557-59.

_____. "Alternate Land Tenure Systems Resulting from Agrarian Reform in Latin America." *Land Economics* 46:3 (August 1970): 215-28.

_____. "Farmers' Organizations in Planning and Implementing Rural Development." In *Rural Development in a Changing World*, pp. 364-90. Edited by Raanan Weitz. Cambridge, Mass.: MIT Press, 1971.

Basu, Kaushik. *The Less Developed Economy: A Critique of Contemporary Theory*. New York: Basil Blackwell, 1984.

Bell, Ian. *The Dominican Republic*. Boulder, Colo.: Westview Press, 1981.

Berry, R. Albert. "Land Reform and the Adequacy of World Food Production." In *International Dimensions of Land Reform*. Edited by J. Montgomery. Boulder, Colo.: Westview Press, 1984.

Berry, R. Albert, and William Cline. *Agrarian Structure and Productivity in Developing Countries*. Baltimore: Johns Hopkins University Press, 1979.

Binswanger, Hans P., and Donald Sillers. "Risk Aversion and Credit Constraints in Farmers' Decision-Making: A Reinterpretation." *Journal of Development Studies* 20 (October 1983): 5-21.

Black, Jan Knippers. *The Dominican Republic: Politics and Development in an Unsovereign State*. Boston: Allen & Unwin, 1986.

Blankstein, C. S., and C. Zuvekas. "Agrarian Reform in Ecuador: An Evaluation of Past Efforts and the Development of a New Approach." *Economic Development and Cultural Change* 22:1 (1973): 73-94.

Bosch, Juan. "Speech on Agrarian Reform." Land Tenure Center files, University of Wisconsin, Madison, 1963.

Brannon, Jeffery, and Eric Baklanoff. "The Political Economy of Agrarian Reform in Yucátan Mexico." *World Development* 12:11/12 (November-December 1984): 1131-41.

Braverman, A., and T. N. Srinivasan. "Credit and Sharecropping in Agrarian Societies." *Journal of Development Economics* 9 (December 1981): 289-312.

Braverman, A., and J. Stiglitz. "Sharecropping and the Interlinking of Agrarian Markets." *American Economic Review* 72 (1982): 695-715.

Bravo-Barros, Carlos. "Informe del Consultor." Proyecto FAO TCP/DOM/2201, 1983.

Calvo, Guillermo A., and Stanislaw Wellisz. "Supervision, Loss of Control, and the Optimum Size of the Firm." *Journal of Political Economy* 86:5 (1978): 943-52.

Carroll, Thomas F. "Group Credit for Small Farmers." *AID Spring Review of Small Farmer Credit*, Vol. XIX, June 1973, No. SR119: 265-82.

_____. "Land Reform Issues in Latin America." In *Latin American Issues: Essays and Comments*. Edited by A. Hirschman. New York: Twentieth Century Fund, 1961.

Carter, Michael R. "Parcelization and Reform Sector Productivity: Theoretical Questions and an Efficient Mixed Institutional Alternative." Working Paper, University of Wisconsin, Madison, 1984a.

_____. "Resource Allocation and Use under Collective Rights and Labour Management in Peruvian Coastal Agriculture." *Economic Journal* 94 (December 1984b): 826-46.

_____. "Risk Sharing and Incentives in the Decollectivization of Agriculture." *Oxford Economic Papers* 39 (1987): 577-95.

Carter, Michael R., and Elena Alvarez. "Changing Paths: The Decollectivization of Agrarian Reform Agriculture in Coastal Peru." 1986 draft of chapter in Thiesenhusen, (1989).

Carter, Michael R., and Don Kanel. "Collective Rice Production in Finca Bermúdez: Institutional Performance and Evolution in the Dominican Agrarian Reform Sector." Land Tenure Center Research Paper No. 83. University of Wisconsin, Madison, 1985.

Castillo, L., and D. Lehmann. "Agrarian Reform and Structural Change in Chile, 1965-79." In *Agrarian Reform in Contemporary Developing Countries*. Edited by A. K. Ghose. New York: St. Martin's Press, 1983.

Cheung, Steven. *The Theory of Share Tenancy*. Chicago: University of Chicago Press, 1969.

Chonchol, Jacques. "Social and Economic Organization of the Chilean Reformed Sector during the Popular Unity Government (1971-September 1973)." In *Cooperative and Commune*, pp. 199-211. Edited by Peter Dorner. Madison: University of Wisconsin Press, 1977.

Clausner, Marlin D. *Rural Santo Domingo: Settled, Unsettled, and Resettled*. Philadelphia: Temple University Press, 1973.

Consejo Nacional de Agricultura (CAPA). "Estudio Sobre el Rol del Estado en la Comercialización del Arroz." Santo Domingo, D.R.: Sercitec-Consultag, 1987.

Costa, Alan Stanley. "Some Developmental Implications of Alternative Land Tenure Systems in the Mexican Pacific-North." Ph.D. Dissertation, University of California, Davis, 1977.

Cox, Paul. "Venezuela's Agrarian Reform at Mid-1977." Land Tenure Center Research Paper No. 71. University of Wisconsin, Madison, 1978.

Crouch, Luis Arturo. *The Development of Capitalism in Dominican Agriculture*. Ph. D. Dissertation, University of California, Berkeley, 1981.

Deere, Carmen D. "A Comparative Analysis of Agrarian Reform in El Salvador and Nicaragua." *Development and Change* 13 (Winter 1982a): 1-41.

———. "Rural Women and State Policy: The Latin American Agrarian Reform Experience." *World Development* 13:9 (September 1985): 1037-53.

DeJanvry, Alain. *The Agrarian Question and Reformism in Latin America*. Baltimore: Johns Hopkins University Press, 1981.

Delgado, Oscar. "Diagnóstico Socio-economico de los Asentamientos Individuales y Colectivos." Proyecto FAO TCP/DOM/2201, 1983.

Deshpande, S. H. *Some Problems of Co-operative Farming*. Bombay: Himalaya Publishing House, 1977.

Domar, Evsey D. "The Soviet Collective Farm as a Producer Cooperative." *American Economic Review* 56:4 (September 1966): 734-57.

Dore y Cabral, Carlos, ed. *Alternativas de Política Agraria*. Santo Domingo: Instituto Tecnológico de Santo Domingo, 1987.

———. *Problemas de la Estructura Agraria Dominicana*. Santo Domingo, 1979.

———. *Reforma Agraria y Luchas Sociales en la República Dominicana 1966-1978*. 2d ed. Santo Domingo, 1981.

Dorner, Peter. *Land Reform and Economic Development*. Kingsport, Tenn.: Penguin Books, 1972.

———, ed. *Cooperatives and Commune: Group Farming in the Economic Development of Agriculture*. Madison: University of Wisconsin Press, 1977.

_____, ed. *Land Reform in Latin America: Issues and Cases*. Land Economics Mono. No. 3. University of Wisconsin, Madison, 1971.

Dorner, Peter, and Don Kanel. "The Economic Case for Land Reform: Employment, Income Distribution and Productivity." In *Land Reform in Latin America*. Edited by P. Dorner. Land Economics Mono. No. 3. University of Wisconsin, Madison, 1971.

Dorner, Peter, and Don Kanel. "Some Economic and Administrative Issues in Group Farming." In *Cooperative and Commune*, pp. 3-16. Edited by Peter Dorner. Madison: University of Wisconsin Press, 1977.

Dorner, P.; C. W. Loomer; R. Penn; and J. Thome. "Agrarian Reform in the Dominican Republic: The Views of Four Consultants." Land Tenure Center Working Paper No. 42. 1967.

Dovring, Folke. "Economic Results of Land Reform." Washington D.C.: Agency for International Development, 1970a.

_____. "Land Reform and Productivity in Mexico." *Land Economics* 46:3 (August 1970b): 264-74.

E.I.U. *Country Report: Cuba, Dominican Republic, Haiti, Puerto Rico, No. 3, 1986*. London: The Economist Publishers, 1986a.

E.I.U. *Country Profile: Dominican Republic, Haiti, Puerto Rico 1986-87*. London: The Economist Publishers, 1986b.

Eckstein, Shlomo. "Land Reform and Cooperative Farming: An Evaluation of the Mexican Experience." In *Rural Development in a Changing World*. Edited by Raanan Weitz. Cambridge, Mass.: MIT Press, 1971.

Eswaran, M., and A. Kotwal. "The Theory of Contractual Structure in Agriculture." *American Economic Review* 75 (1985): 352-67.

Feder, Ernest. *The Rape of the Peasantry: Latin America's Landholding System*. Garden City: Doubleday & Co., 1971.

Figueroa, Adolfo. "Agrarian Reforms in Latin America: A Framework and an Instrument of Rural Development." *World Development* 5:1/2 (1977): 155-68.

Flores, Edmundo. "Issues of Land Reform." *Journal of Political Economy* 78:4 (July-August 1970): 890-905.

Food and Agriculture Organization. "Mexico—Country Review Paper." *Land Reform, Land Settlement, and Cooperatives* (1980)1/2: 79-88.

Food and Agriculture Organization. "Ecuador—Country Review Paper." *Land Reform, Land Settlement, and Cooperatives* (1980)1/2: 89-99.

French, Jerome. "Analysis of Organizational Aspects of Small Farmer Credit Programs." *AID Spring Review of Small Farmer Credit*, Vol. XIX, June 1973, No. SR119: 237-61.

Furtado, Celso. *Economic Development of Latin America*. Translated by Suzette Macedo. New York: Cambridge University Press, 1976.

Galeski, Boguslaw. "The Models of Collective Farming." In *Cooperative and Commune*, pp. 17-42. Edited by Peter Dorner. Madison: The University of Wisconsin Press, 1977.

Genao, Hipólito, and Alfonso Torres. "Funcionamiento de la Administración y Posibilidades de Autogestión en las Fincas Asociativas 'Bermúdez A' y 'El Esfuerzo' de la Reforma Agraria en la Provincia Valverde." Thesis for the title Ingeniero Agrónomo, Instituto Superior de Agricultura, 1987.

Gleijeses, Piero. *The Dominican Crisis: The 1965 Constitutionalist Revolt and American Intervention*. Translated by Lawrence Lipson. Baltimore: Johns Hopkins University Press, 1978.

Graber, Eric. "Strategy, Policies and Programs for Economic Growth and Social Progress in the Dominican Republic: With Reference to Rural Development." Ph.D. Dissertation, Iowa State University, 1978.

Grindle, Merilee S. *State and Countryside: Development Policy and Agrarian Politics in Latin America*. Baltimore: Johns Hopkins University Press, 1986.

Groves, Theodore. "Incentives in Teams." *Econometrica* 41:4 (July 1973): 617-31.

Gutiérrez, Ana Teresa. "Asociación de Agricultores Sergio Abigail Cabrera, Inc." Santiago, D.R.: ISA, 1983a.

_____. "El Asentamiento Campesino Vásquez Quintero." Santiago, D.R.: ISA, 1983b.

Guzmán, Fernando. "Ambito Jurídico Institutional: Marcha La Reforma Agraria Dominicana Hacia una Nueva Reordenación Institucional?" Land Tenure Center, University of Wisconsin, Madison, 1983.

Hall, Carolyn. *Costa Rica: A Geographical Interpretation in Historical Perspective*. Boulder, Colo.: Westview Press, 1985.

Harris, Milton, and Artur Raviv. "Optimal Incentive Contracts with Imperfect Information." *Journal of Economic Theory* 20 (1979): 231-59.

Hirschman, Albert O., *Journeys Toward Progress: Studies of Economic Policy-Making in Latin America*. New York: Twentieth Century Fund, 1963.

_____, ed. *Latin American Issues: Essays and Comments*. New York: Twentieth Century Fund, 1961.

Holmstrom, Bengt. "Moral Hazard and Observability." *Bell Journal of Economics* 10:1 (1979): 74-91.

Horton, Douglas E. "Land Reform and Group Farming in Peru." In *Co-operative and Commune*, pp. 213-38. Edited by Peter Dorner. Madison: University of Wisconsin Press, 1977.

Kanel, Don. "Size of Farm and Economic Development." *Indian Journal of Agricultural Economics* 22 (April-June 1967): 26-44.

Kay, Cristóbal. "Achievements and Contradictions of the Peruvian Agrarian Reform." *Journal of Development Studies* (January 1982): 141-70.

King, Russell. *Land Reform: A World Survey*. Boulder, Colo.: Westview Press, 1977.

Kotwal, Ashok. "The Role of Consumption Credit in Agricultural Tenancy." *Journal of Development Economics* 18 (1985): 273-95.

Liboreiro, Ernesto S. "The Small Farmer in the Context of Agrarian Reform and Rural Development in Latin America and the Caribbean." *Land Reform, Land Settlement, and Cooperatives* (1979) 1: 80-97.

Lipton, Michael. "Agricultural Finance and Rural Credit in Poor Countries." *World Development* 4:7 (July 1976): 543-53.

Lundahl, Mats. *Peasants and Poverty: A Study of Haiti*. New York: St. Martin's Press, 1979.

Marinez, Pablo A. *Resistencia Campesina, Imperialismo y Reforma Agraria en R.D.*, 1st ed. Santo Domingo: Ediciones CEPAE, 1984.

Marschak, J., and R. Radner. *The Economic Theory of Teams*. New Haven: Yale University Preess, 1972.

Mears, Leon Glenn. *The Dominican Republic: Agriculture and Trade*. Washington, D.C.: U. S. Dept. of Agriculture, 1963.

Mellor, J. W. *Economics of Agricultural Development*. Ithaca, N.Y.: Cornell University Press, 1966.

Mirrlees, James A. "The Optimal Structure of Incentives and Authority within an Organization." *Bell Journal of Economics* 7:1 (Spring 1976): 105-31.

Montgomery, John D., ed. *International Dimensions of Land Reform*. Boulder, Colo.: Westview Press, 1984.

Moya Pons, Frank. *Manual de Historia Dominicana*. 4th ed. Santiago, D.R.: Universidad Católica Madre y Maestra, 1978.

Munguía, George Anthony. "A Transitional Stage in the Agricultural Sector: The Case of the Dominican Republic." Ph.D. Dissertation, Fordham University, New York, 1975.

_____. "Asentamientos Colectivos Fincas Estatales y Economías de Escala." *Estudios Sociales*, Vol. 9, No. 7, 1976.

Newbery, David. "The Choice of Rental Contract in Peasant Agriculture." In *Agriculture in Development Theory*, pp. 109-37. Edited by L. G. Reynolds. New Haven, Conn.: Yale University Press, 1975.

Oi, Walter and E. Clayton. "A Peasant's View of a Soviet Collective Farm." *American Economic Review* 58:1 (1968): 37-59.

Peterson, Robert, E. Daniel, and R. Battles. "Agrarian Reform and Agricultural Credit in the Dominican Republic." Rural Dev. Division AID, LA/ID, 1965.

Putterman, Louis. "A Modified Collective Agriculture in Rural Growth-with-Equity: Reconsidering the Private Unimodal Solution." *World Development* 11 (1983): 77-100.

_____. "On Optimality in Collective Institutional Choice." *Journal of Comparative Economics* 5 (1981): 392-403.

_____. "Voluntary Collectivization: A Model of Producers' Institutional Choice." *Journal of Comparative Economics* 4 (1980): 125-57.

Putterman, Louis, and Marie DiGiorgio. "Choice and Efficiency in a Model of Democratic Semi-Collective Agriculture." *Oxford Economic Papers* 37 (1985): 1-21.

Quibria, M. G., and Salim Rashid. "The Puzzle of Sharecropping: A Survey of Theories." *World Development* 12:2 (1984): 103-14.

Rodríguez, Francisco. *El Impacto Económico de la Reforma Agraria en R.D. 1977-1982*. Santo Domingo, 1984.

Rodríguez-Núñez, Pablo. "A Socioeconomic Evaluation of Rice Producing Asentamientos in the Agrarian Reform Sector of the Dominican Republic." Land Tenure Center, University of Wisconsin, Madison, 1983.

_____. "Veinte Años de Arroz y Reforma Agraria en la República Dominicana: 1963-1983." Land Tenure Center, University of Wisconsin, Madison, 1985.

Rodríguez-Núñez, Pablo, L. Colono, J. Ogando, R. Stringer, and W. Thiesenhusen. "Agrarian Reform in the Dominican Republic: The Case of Ysura." Land Tenure Center, University of Wisconsin Madison, 1983.

Ruhl, J. Mark. "Agrarian Structure and Political Stability in Honduras." *Journal of Inter-American Studies and World Affairs* 26:1 (1984): 33-68.

Safilios-Rothschild, Constantina. "Women and the Agrarian Reform in Honduras." *Land Reform, Land Settlement, and Cooperatives* (1983) 1/2: 15-24.

Schiller, Otto. *Cooperation and Integration in Agricultural Production*. Bombay: Asia Publishing House, 1969.

_____. "Organization of Rural Cooperation in Developing Countries." In *Rural Development in a Changing World*. Edited by Raanan Weitz. Cambridge, Mass.: MIT Press, 1971.

Schultz, Theodore. *Transforming Traditional Agriculture*. New Haven: Yale University Press, 1964.

Schwinden, James, and G. Feaster. "The INCORA Supervised Credit Program." *AID Spring Review of Small Farmer Credit*, Vol. V, February 1973, No. SR105 Country Papers.

Secretaría del Estado de Agricultura (SEA). *Plan Operativa 1987*. Santo Domingo, D.R.

Seligson, Mitchell A. "The Impact of Agrarian Reform: A Study of Costa Rica." *Journal of Development Areas* 13 (January 1979): 161-74.

Sen, Amartya. "Labour Allocation in a Cooperative Enterprise." *Review of Economic Studies* 33 (1966): 361-71.

Sexto Censo Nacional Agropecuario 1971. 2d ed. Secretariado Técnico de la Presidencia, Oficina Nacional de Estadística, República Dominicana.

Shavell, Steven. "Risk Sharing and Incentives in the Principal and Agent Relationship." *Bell Journal of Economics* (1979): 55-73.

Stanfield, David. "Agrarian Reform in the Dominican Republic." 1986 draft of chapter in Thiesenhusen, 1989.

Stanfield, David, C. Dore y Cabral, P. Rodríguez-Núñez, B. Ferreiras, V. Lambert, L. Suarez, and R. Stringer. "Evolving Property Relations in the Agrarian Reform of the Dominican Republic." Revised edition of paper presented at L.A.S.A. Meeting, Boston, Mass., 1986.

Stanfield, David, and D. Kaimowitz. "The Organization of Production Units in the Nicaraguan Agrarian Reform." Prepared for the 26th Annual Convention of the International Studies Assoc. in Washington D.C., 1985.

Stanfield, David, P. Rodríguez-Núñez, L. Colón, J. Ogando, L. E. Pérez Cuevas, J. Zarzuela, M. Carter, R. Stringer, and D. Kanel. "An Inquiry into the Management Models Used in the Agrarian Reform Asentamientos." Land Tenure Center, University of Wisconsin, Madison, 1983.

Stavenhagen, Rodolfo. "Land Reform and Institutional Alternatives in Agriculture: The Case of the Mexican Ejido." Institute for Development Occasional Paper No. 9, Vienna, 1973.

Stiglitz, Joseph E. "Incentives and Risk Sharing in Sharecropping." *Review of Economic Studies* 41 (April 1974): 219-55.

_____. "Incentives, Risk and Information: Notes Towards a Theory of Hierarchy." *Bell Journal of Economics* 6:2 (1975): 552-79.

Strasma, John, P. Gore, and J. Nash. *Agrarian Reform in El Salvador.* Washington, D.C.: Checchi & Co, 1983.

Stringer, Randy. "Innovations in Group Farming: The Case of Sergio Abagail Cabrera in the Dominican Republic." Land Tenure Center Research Paper No. 82. University of Wisconsin, Madison, 1986.

Tai, Hung-Chao. *Land Reform & Politics: A Comparative Analysis.* Berkeley: University of California Press, 1974.

Tejo J., Pedro. "Avances de la Reforma Agraria y del Desarrollo Rural en la República Dominicana." Food and Agriculture Organization, 1983.

Thome, Joseph R. "The Agrarian Reform in the Dominican Republic: Problems and Perspectives." Land Tenure Center, University of Wisconsin, Madison, 1967.

Thiesenhusen, William C. "The Illusory Goal of Equity in Latin American Agrarian Reform." In *International Dimensions of Land Reform.* Edited by J. Montgomery. Boulder, Colo.: Westview Press, 1984.

_____. *Searching for Agrarian Reform in Latin America.* Winchester, Mass.: Allen & Unwin, 1989.

Tinnermeier, Ronald L. "Technology, Profit, and Agricultural Credit." *AID Spring Review of Small Farmer Credit,* Vol. XIX, June 1973, No. SR119: 93-111.

United States Department of Agriculture. "Dominican Republic." Western Hemisphere Branch, Economic Research Service, 1961.

Ward, Benjamin. "The Firm in Illyria: Market Syndicalism" *American Economic Review* 48:4 (1958): 566-89.

Warriner, Doreen. *Land Reform in Principle and Practice.* Oxford University Press, 1969.

_____. "Results of Land Reform in Asian and Latin American Countries." *Food Research Institute Studies* 12:2 (1973): 115-32.

Weil, Thomas E., J. Black, H. Blutstein, K. Johnston, D. McMorris, F. Munson. *Area Handbook for the Dominican Republic.* Washington, D.C.: American University Press, 1973.

Weitz, Raanan. *Rural Development in a Changing World.* Cambridge, Mass.: MIT Press, 1971.

Weitzman, Martin L. "The New Soviet Incentive Model." *Bell Journal of Economics* 7:1 (Spring 1976): 251-57.

Wiarda, Howard J., and Michael Kryzanek. *The Dominican Republic: A Caribbean Crucible.* Boulder, Colo.: Westview Press, 1982.

Wilkie, James. *Measuring Land Reform Supplement to Statistical Abstract.* Los Angeles: UCLA Latin American Center, 1974.

Williamson, Oliver E. "Hierarchical Control and Optimum Firm Size." *Journal of Political Economy* (April 1967): 123-38.

World Bank. *Dominican Republic: Economic Prospects and Policies to Renew Growth*. Report No. 4735-DO, 1984.

Zuvekas, Clarence. "Land Tenure, Income, and Employment in Rural Haiti: A Survey." U.S. AID mimeo, Washington, D.C., 1978.

Index

ABOUT THE AUTHOR

CARRIE A. MEYER, raised on a farm in Illinois, received a Ph.D. in economics from the University of Illinois at Champaign-Urbana, after serving as a Peace Corps volunteer in the Dominican Republic. Currently she is an assistant professor of economics at George Mason University in Fairfax, Virginia, teaching economic development and microeconomic theory.